Mary M. (Mary Miller) Meline

In six months or The two friends

Mary M. (Mary Miller) Meline

In six months or The two friends

ISBN/EAN: 9783741134999

Manufactured in Europe, USA, Canada, Australia, Japa

Cover: Foto ©Andreas Hilbeck / pixelio.de

Manufactured and distributed by brebook publishing software (www.brebook.com)

Mary M. (Mary Miller) Meline

In six months or The two friends

IN SIX MONTHS;

OR,

THE TWO FRIENDS.

BY

MARY M. MELIÑE,

Authoress of the "Montargeş Legacy."

BALTIMORE:
KELLY, PIET AND COMPANY,
No. 174 W. Baltimore St.
1874.

L'ENVOI.

"Go, little book, from this my solitude!
 I cast thee on the waters—go thy ways!
 And if, as I believe, thy vein be good,
 The world will find thee after many days."

SOUTHEY.

IVYWALL, *Washington, July,* 1871.

To the

REVERED AND BELOVED FRIEND

OF THE WRITER'S LIFETIME,

Most Rev. Jno. B. Purcell, Archbishop of Cincinnati

THIS LITTLE BOOK

IS MOST RESPECTFULLY DEDICATED.

IN SIX MONTHS;

OR,

THE TWO FRIENDS.

PART FIRST.

CHAPTER I.

THE TWO FRIENDS.

NIGHT had settled over the earth after an intensely hot day in August, 1867. There had been not even a breath of air since morning; the atmosphere had been stifling, but as the sun went down a light, refreshing wind sprang up, and nature seemed to hold herself awake for a while to drink in the revivifying zephyr, ere she closed her petals, and drew her green robes closer abouther in preparation for her night of rest. Presently, an immense globe of pale white light shot up out of a pile of clouds in the east, as if from an enormous cannon, and the heavens were irradiated, and the waters of the silent river gleamed and glistened, and rippled along beneath arrows of silvery sheen. Diana had asserted her sovereignty, and not even Venus, from her western throne, dared dispute her claim.

Louis Gwynne had been enjoying the *dolce far niente* of the hour, stretched upon a *chaise longue,* and smoking a nargileh out on the balcony on which his apartments opened. He was a very luxurious and comfort-loving youth, and looked, as the soft summer air toyed with the chestnut curls clustering closely over his head, his large, dark eyes veiled by their heavily fringed lids, and his classic features relaxed in the repose of his perfect enjoyment, a very Antinous taking his rest under the summer night of Greece.

Wealthy, and handsome beyond the usual beauty of most men—one of our heroes is before us—" lord of himself, that heritage of woe," at the age of twenty-five. His father was still living, and possessed of a large fortune, but Louis had been early independent of him by the bequest of a bachelor god-father, who, dying when his god-son was a boy of ten, had bequeathed to him all his property, real and personal; the which bequest had nearly doubled itself before Louis had attained his majority. His mother had died when he was about six years old, leaving a baby girl, Eleanore, whose helpless infancy seemed to appeal with a stronger claim to his and his father's affection, from her loss.

Never had this most sacred, but alas, so often profaned and neglected tie, been guarded so perfectly, and sustained so beautifully, as between this brother and sister.

That his independence was not a "heritage of woe," was owing to the natural refinement of soul and mind, the true spirit of "*noblesse oblige*" inherited from his parents, and the influence of his affection for his young sister, whose soft, dove-like eyes rose fondly, pleading between him and many a strong temptation.

That we may more fully understand his character, let us glance around the apartment, the windows of which open to the floor, shaded by costly lace curtains through which a subdued light gleams from a shaded lamp.

The floor is covered with matting, and the furniture with its summer robes of chintz, but the chairs and sofas are all of the most luxurious and inviting shapes and styles. The walls are covered with fine pictures, copies of the old masters and originals by the new, engravings and etchings, all of subjects showing a refinement and delicacy of mind rather singular among the *jeunesses dorees* of the present day. Above the mantle-piece is a copy of Carlo Dolce's exquisite "Mother and Child," on either side, Thorwalden's "Night and Morning." In the recess to the right of the fireplace is a collection of pipes of all kinds, nargilehs, meerschaums, churchwardens, arranged fancifully upon the wall. In the other recess a number of swords hang, all different, from the yataghan of the Mussel-man to the French court-dress sword. Several statuettes rest upon carved brackets; here, a small Greek slave, there, a copy of the same sculptor's exquisite "Silence," on another, "Sabrina fair" rested, listening to the voice that had called her from her coral palace; on the marble slab beneath the long mirror, which hangs between the windows, is a copy of that marvellous piece of ancient art, the "Laocoon." A book-case half opened revealed its choice treasures, and on a music stand beside it lay a silver flute. Tables and stands of ormolu or marble are covered with books or handsome artistic trifles, and masculine confusion reigns supreme, yet while a woman's hand is needed to restore things to a state more in accordance with Nature's *First Law*, there is nothing that could offend the purest feminine taste or eye.

Upon a table in the centre of the room stands the organd burner, with its green, porcelain shade, and just where the light falls strongest is a bust of Clytie; not the Clytie ordinarily seen, with the leaves forming a frame for her lovely shoulders—in this, the face is of an exquisite Greek profile, the hair thrown back from the low forehead, falls in a wreath of foliage over the small ears, thus forming a coronet for the beautiful brow. It had been the work of a young artist whom Gwynne had met in Florence, and had drawn his attention for two reasons; one, the beautiful conception, so perfectly unique; the other, the striking likeness he discovered to his beloved Eleanore.

But while we have been describing him and his surroundings, Louis has shaken off the *far niente* spirit, and risen from his lounging attitude, displaying a figure taller than the common height of men, supple and lithe, and fully developed, and a fitting accompaniment to the head and face that sat so proudly on his shoulders.

"By Jove!" he exclaimed, "what a lovely night! and just the time for a row in the

'Zephyr.' If I only had the moral courage to transport myself to Hudson's Bay for the next six weeks to escape this broiling heat! But 'Home, Sweet Home,' and I am very lazy."

And whistling the air to the song, the first words of which he had quoted, he threw a light overcoat over his arm, put on his hat, and lighting a cigar, left the room.

As he descended the stairs, he was met by a figure springing up them three steps at a time.

"Gwynne, old boy!"

"Ed., by all that's marvellous!"

"Even I, amico!"

"What brings you from Boston?"

"'A truant disposition, good my lord,' I might answer truly."

"Well, I say, this is jolly! I was just about to seek solace for my solitude in the 'Zephyr,' but as soon as you have refreshed yourself we can go together."

"I need no refreshment, Luigi, having been in the city since six o'clock, and having had a bath and dinner at the Burnet House, so I am ready for anything you may propose."

"Well, let us have a look at you by the gaslight, and sit down awhile and talk. It is not late, and we'll have plenty of time an hour hence for a boatride before the moon sets," replied Gwynne, leading the way back to the room.

Edgar Mainwaring had neither the physical beauty nor grace of manner which was so charming in Louis Gwynne; he was quiet, retiring, and reticent, except to his friend. While his features lacked regularity, and, therefore, could not be classified or criticized by any regular rules, there was a beauty about his face all its own, and none the less there, that one could not say in what it consisted. Perhaps it was the noble soul looking out of the large, blue eyes, which, with their long lashes, and the evenly-marked brows above them, had a "shadowy depth" in their expression which was very charming. Perhaps it was in the masses of dark brown hair falling in waves (it did not curl as Gwynne's did) over his finely developed and intellectual forehead, or it might have been in the winning smile of the rather large mouth—unquestionably, it was there.

Mainwaring was an orphan. He had been sent at an early age to Harvard, and there, meeting Gwynne, a warm friendship had sprung up between them. They were friends in more than the common acceptation of the word, loving each other with a love passing that of brothers; a love whose tenderness and depth had more of woman's nature than of man's; a love, the sunshine of which, up to this moment, had been clouded by no unkind thought, word, or deed, chilled by no breath of doubt or suspicion.

In their classes and studies they were always together, although Gwynne's rare facility of acquirement made light work of the most difficult tasks, which necessitated strict application and study on the part of his less gifted friend. But what Mainwaring learned he did not readily forget, a faculty upon which Gwynne was glad sometimes to rely.

When the war broke out, just after they had graduated, they enlisted in the same regiment, were promoted together in it, both escaped unwounded in many a fierce combat, and when the strife was over, laid aside their swords on the same day.

After that their lives were necessarily apart.

Gwynne's fortune abrogated the necessity for any exertion, while Mainwaring's small patrimony barely afforded him a support. Besides, his was not the luxury-loving nature of Gwynne's; he turned to work gladly for its own sake.

He had neither brother nor sister, but an uncle who was a prominent lawyer in Boston offered him a sort of partnership in his business, of which offer he gladly availed himself, and a home beneath his roof. His uncle having a client who had a claim to some property in England and Scotland, thinking it would be a good opportunity for Edgar to see a little of the world, proposed sending him abroad for a year; to get through the business as soon as possible and having the rest of his time his own, to see as much or as little of the continent as he cared to. Having made all his arrangements for starting on a certain date, he had sought his friend to say good-bye.

"I have half a mind to go with you, Ed.," said Gwynne, as Mainwaring paused in his account of his plans.

"Make it a whole one and go!" exclaimed Mainwaring, eagerly catching at the idea.

"It is very tempting. I wish I could!"

"Oh, Louis, don't hesitate. Think what it will be to go over those old-time places together! What in the world can prevent you? You have neither claims nor duties, you fortunate fellow.

"Let me see, this is Tuesday, Wednesday, Thursday, Friday, Sat—yes, it's sudden, but I'll do it. Yes! I'll go!"

"You dear, old fellow! How jolly it will be!"

"Yes," replied Louis, "let us enjoy ourselves. I was going anyhow in May to bring Eleanore from Vevai, where, you know, she has been at school for the last three years. But I can go now and spend the rest of the summer among the Alps. Do you go to France?"

"I shall be kept in England very nearly six months, I fancy; you can spend them with me just as well."

"I hate England," ejaculated Gwynne.

"Why?"

"Can't say especially, Dr. Fell, and that sort of thing, you know; and I hate England."

"Well, you can wait for me in Paris and we will 'do' the Continent together."

"I can't promise to wait for you in Paris, but I will meet you somewhere—say, Cologne, if you will—at the end of six months. I promised Eleanore to give her a sight of the lions when she left her *pension;* the little girl thought it very hard that I left her a prisoner at school and went myself to Italy when I took her over; but I consoled her by telling her I was only qualifying myself for becoming her *cicerone*, and when we went together I'd know better what was worth seeing, and what not, than if it were also my first experience."

"You're a funny fellow, Louis! Have you never felt a touch of the 'tender passion?' never met a woman to share your heart with your sister, or rob her of it altogether?"

"Never! And what's more, my dear boy, I don't think I ever shall! Certainly not while society is as it is! Why, who among the butterflies of fashion who flutter their gaudy wings under the midnight gas, or fill our streets to be gazed at and to gaze —where among them could a man who wished to *live* find a helpmeet?"

"So you want a plain, quiet little body, who doesn't dance, doesn't care for society, only darns your stockings, and keeps your dressing-gown and slippers ready for you, and always looks perfectly well dressed in a grey merino frock, with white linen collar and cuffs and blue ribbon bow, as in novels."

"No such thing! I adore beauty; therefore my wife must be beautiful—a queenly woman, full of all gracious sweetness; one who enjoys her life and lives it. She may dance to her heart's content, and if she does it well, no one will delight more in helping her than I. She may enjoy society, and must know how to hold her own in it; she must be perfect mistress of the '*savoir faire*,' but she must not let society claim all her duty. As for her intellectual acquirements, I shall want a companion and friend as well as a wife; and as for her heart and affections, she must be a true woman—*voilà tout!* As for the stocking darning—well, that shall be a matter of taste, not of requirement; for, as far as I can see now, there will be no need for any such industry. In short, my wife must be 'not too good for human nature's daily food,' but she must be as different from the girl of the period as it is possible. Dost thou like the picture?"

"Much. But I question your ability to find the reality."

"So do I; and for that reason I have not sought it. If I thought Eleanore would ever be like the rest, I'd bury her alive in a convent!"

"Softly, softly! You talk, my dear fellow, as if you were Autocrat of all the Russias, a nine-tailed Bashaw, and President of the United States, in one. Young ladies are not so easily buried alive now as in the days of 'Marmion,' and generally have a good deal to say for themselves."

"True. I can only regret the progress of the age and my own impotence," said Gwynne, laughing.

"You propose going to Italy. *Apropos*, Garibaldi seems to be to the fore again, and it is likely Pio Nono will not be quite so tranquil as he has been; how about that?"

"Oh! if there is any fighting, I will keep quietly out of it, and go somewhere else."

"Then you have no generous desire to help the Italians in their struggles for freedom—their noble efforts to throw off the trammels of the priesthood."

"Not much. While I wish them goodspeed and success to their efforts, our own war perfectly satisfied my combative propensities for all time."

"Well, I confess to a great longing to draw a sword in the good cause; to add my little strength to the mighty power which is slowly but surely upheaving the weight which is to fall with annihilating force upon the abominations of Romanism and its right hand, Jesuitism."

"Yes," said Gwynne, yawning, "it would be very jolly to see Victor Emmanuel, or Garibaldi, seated in the Vatican or Quirinal, scattering the treasures of the Church right and left. Wouldn't they make things fly? and wouldn't there be weeping and gnashing of teeth among the children of the 'Mighty Mother.' They are welcome to do all they can—I shall not hinder—but I most certainly will not help."

"What have you been reading lately?" asked Mainwaring, getting up to look at a book which lay open upon the table in the lamp-light.

"Nothing very new. Renan's Life of Jesus."

"Ah!" exclaimed Mainwaring with gusto, as if he were rolling a choice morsel under his tongue. "What a treat you have in store if you have never read it! It is grand!"

"How grand?" asked Gwynne. "The style, I grant you, is very fascinating and finished. But the subject! He has written one continuous blasphemy!"

"You don't mean to say you don't endorse him?"

"Most assuredly I do not!"

"Why, my dear fellow, how can you refuse to acknowledge the truth of his conclusions?"

"Because I am not an infidel, Ed."

"Neither am I—far from it. One can retain his belief in a God without elevating a man to the Godhead."

"My dear boy, it is too warm to argue the question—have it your own way. I dare say, if Boston has decided that Renan's idea is gospel, the world will follow suit; and, of course, if all the world think so, I will, too; the world is always right if Boston leads the way," he added, rising and throwing his arm over Mainwaring's shoulder caressingly, and by the gesture taking away any sting his words might carry.

Mainwaring paused an instant, then his face relaxed into a smile, and he grasped Gwynne's hand.

"You are the same old fellow, Luigi, and it is impossible to be angry with you. But what have we here?" he continued, picking up the Clytie.

"A new conception of an old story, Ed., which I found by accident in Florence, in one of my rambles among the less famous studios. Don't you like it?"

"Like it? Why, it is exquisite! But I confess I do not recognize it."

"Not the Clytie!"

"Oh, I see—yes, the idea is beautiful—ah, amico, how happy you ought to be, able as you are to gratify every æsthetic taste so readily."

"And I am happy, Edgar. I believe I am as happy as it is possible to be. I haven't a care upon my mind nor a wish of my heart ungratified. Why I am thus indulged by the Power that rules this mundane sphere, I am unable to say, but the fact remains. And, now, what do you say to the 'Zephyr'?"

"All right. I am ready."

They left the house and passed under the overhanging trees along the path towards the river. Rolla, a Newfoundland dog, sprang up from a side porch as he caught sight of the two figures, gave a warning bark, then recognized his master, and in two ungainly leaps was at his side, springing up at him to force acknowledgment of his presence.

"Boat, Rollo! boat!" said Gwynne, and the dog sprang away from him and was at the boat-house door in a moment.

While Gwynne undid the fastening of the boat-house, Mainwaring sat upon a bench near the shore, gazing in silent thought upon the lovely scene, while the dog busied himself hunting for something along the bank. When they got into the boat and shoved off, Rolla plunged into the water and swam some distance after them, barking his loudest, but soon tiring of this amusement, he returned to the shore and left the friends to their own devices.

Both were silent as they rowed up the stream to a point where, at a turn of the river, the city lay before them. The "Queen of the West" lay quiet under her smoky canopy, with her coronet of hills; and the Ohio, flowing steadily past her footstool, reflected the lights from houses close to the banks.

Just as they rested a moment, the locomotive and its attendant train rushed along the iron road close to the shore, and in the dim light seemingly in the very water, and as it sped on its way, waking the echoes on either side with its shrill whistle, it left a brilliant cataract of sparks that danced for a few seconds in the air, then sank to meet their reflection in the water.

They paused for a little while to take in the picture, and then the boat was headed down the stream, and Gwynne, drawing in his oars, changed his seat for one nearer Edgar, who held the rudder, and let the craft float gently on.

It was a lovely sight, that beautiful river in the silvery moonlight. The hills in Kentucky were mostly covered with trees; but lights gleamed from the houses dotting the sides of those on the Ohio bank, while the moonlight threw a glamour of most softening effect over their rugged and dismantled aspect. Neither steamboat nor locomotive disturbed the peacefulness of the scene. Nature had it all in her own hands, and a most perfect picture she made of it.

Neither Mainwaring nor Gwynne were in a mood for talk, but Edgar said, softly:

" 'Drifting,' Louis. 'Tis just the time and place."

And presently Gwynne's rich voice broke the stillness:

>My soul to-day
>Is far away
>Sailing the Vesuvian Bay,
>My winged boat,
>A bird afloat,
>Skims round the purple peaks remote.

>Round purple peaks
>It sails, and seeks
>Blue inlets and their crystal creeks
>Where high rocks throw
>Through deeps below
>A duplicated golden glow.

>Here Ischia smiles
>O'er liquid miles,
>And yonder, bluest of the isles,
>Calm Capri waits,
>Her sapphire gates
>Beguiling to her bright estates.

>I heed not if
>My rippling skiff
>Floats swift or slow from cliff to cliff;
>With dreamful eyes
>My spirit lies
>Under the walls of Paradise.

The day so mild
Is heaven's own child,
With earth and ocean reconciled;
The airs I feel
Around me steal
Are murmuring to the murmuring keel.

Over the rail
My hand I trail
Within the shadow of the sail;
A joy intense,
The cooling sense
Glides down my drowsy indolence.

No more, no more
The worldly shore
Upbraids me with its loud uproar!
With dreamful eyes
My spirit lies
Under the walls of Paradise!

Two weeks later the friends parted in London. They arranged to meet that day six months at Cologne and, the better to enjoy their reunion, to hold no communication with each other by letter, but to leave all chance adventures, all account of what they should see and hear and do, for a *viva vôce* recital at the time of reunion.

PART SECOND.

CHAPTER I.

LETTERS OF EDGAR MAINWARING.

LONDON, Sept. 9th, 1867.

DEAR LOUIS:

YOUR *dèbonnaire* face with its frame of the railroad car window haunts me sadly. I want you, Louis, at my side again, and already regret the foolish arrangement which cuts us off from all intercourse with each other for six months.

But I must not lose my time in vain regrets; to-morrow I shall begin operations; presenting my credentials, etc.

I now realize something of what a London fog is. Ye powers! The density of it!

My journal, Louis, is to be in the form of letters; if I cannot mail them to you, it will be some satisfaction, and seem to bring us more closely together, to write them.

Sept. 10th.—I had written thus much, when your friend, Maitland, knocked at my door; he had kindly come to cheer my loneliness. We sat and smoked and talked until quite late, when he rose to leave me, telling me he would call the next day and be my guide about the city.

Sept. 11th.—I have been busy all day upon the preliminaries of my work. So far, I have had nothing to complain of, having met only courtesy and promises of assistance. Maitland has just come in, and proposes to show me London by gaslight, as a phase of existence to which nothing with us, even in New York, "*si parva licet componere magnis*," can afford a parallel.

October 1st.—My dear Louis:—Nearly three weeks since I have been able to hold a pen. I did see London by gaslight with a vengeance! We sauntered along, hardly noticing how far we had gone, until Maitland remarked that we had crossed Holburn and were in St. Giles. You have read of, if you have never been in, this section of the great city, but no pen can give a true idea of the reality. Gin palaces blazed at nearly every corner; stalls of petty merchandise were still opened upon the pavement; poor, miserable women, and wretched men and fearful-looking children, swarmed and quarreled and elbowed each other, until, in sickening disgust, I was about to beg Maitland to lead me out of the district as quickly as possible, when the door of one of the gin palaces was thrown open, and a woman reeled or was flung out upon the pavement. A man followed her, and, with a frightful oath, gave a brutal kick to the prostrate form. Obeying my natural impulse, I sprang forward and pushed the fellow away; in another instant, the door behind us opened again and several men came to the assistance of the first. I have a dim recollection of a swaying to and fro of angry, brutal faces, but little else, until I opened my eyes one morning and found Maitland bending anxiously over me, saying:

"That's right, old fellow! Now we'll do nicely!"

I immediately demanded to know the extent of my injuries.

"Nothing to signify, considering what a squire of dames you are," laughed Maitland. "Item, a broken head, ditto arm; item, a cut over the forehead, which, had it been a little more on the temple, would have most effectually put a stop to all future rescues of down-trodden females."

He spoke lightly, but I could see he was anxious, and as I felt myself turning deathly sick and closed my eyes, he rang the bell hastily and sent his man for the doctor, who had left orders to that effect if the least bad symptom appeared upon my return to consciousness.

It was some time before I was able to sit up at all, and to-day I have written this at intervals, propped up by pillows. I hope to progress to an easy chair next week, and after that is accomplished all will, I trust, go well.

Oct. 4th.—This is Sunday and my first day in an easy chair. The busy life of

London is stilled, and even over the foggy air a "Sabbath quiet," falls. I have thought much of you, Louis, *amico mio,* and wondered what you were doing and where you might be. Have you reached the goal of your hopes—Rome? Things look "squally" —as we say over the water—for the "Holy Father." Liberty and progress are making great strides even in Italy, and it may be that in this our day, Louis, will be seen their final triumph over priestcraft and ignorance.

I wish I could tell you into what kind hands I have fallen. They have proved themselves good Samaritans truly in every sense of the word. You must know that at present "everybody" is out of town. Sir George and Lady Maitland were among the everybodies until they heard of my accident, and then, though perfect strangers to me, they returned to nurse me. Maitland himself expected to have left for Scotland the last week in September, but stays "for fear I'd be lonesome."

CHAPTER II.

OCTOBER 11th.—I am afraid, amico, when you read this the tables will be turned. I, you will say, who so often called you "dreamer," am growing fanciful—and fanciful over what? The last thing anyone who knows me would think of—a cross! And this was the way of it:

The house of the Maitlands is situated in a charming part of Kensington. Trees had been planted years ago when the street was first opened, and now shade it delightfully, while opposite to the house is a park, one of those oases found here and there in the midst of the dusty, busy city. Owing to the shade of the trees, the leaves not having all fallen yet, much that goes on in the streets is hidden from my view; but clear against the sky, far up, raised above the tree-tops and the smoke by the graceful spire gleams a gilded cross, and regularly three times a day the sweet-toned bells of a church are rung. Kind and attentive as the family are, I am necessarily much alone, and since I have been able to sit up I have varied my amusement from books and papers by watching the changing leaves, building *chateaux en Espagne,* and studying the tableaux presented by the different groupings of the clouds around the cross.

Yesterday Maitland was sitting with me, when I drew his attention to some cloud shapes which had clustered in a particularly fantastical way, seeming at the foot of my cross.

"Yes," replied he, "very fine; pity the building belongs to the sect it does—Roman Catholics."

"I judged so from the ringing of the bells so regularly."

"It is a new church," continued Maitland, "built since the new dogma, which Pius IX has trumped up at Rome with the help of the Jesuits, has been added to the one, *unchangeable* Faith, and named after it —the Church of the Immaculate Conception, or the Immaculata, I don't know which."

"What was the general opinion here in England on the subject of that 'definition,' as the Romanists call it?" I asked.

"You have given me a wide field," he replied, laughing. "'Here in England.' I can only speak from my own experience and reading. The 'definition' was greeted with considerable surprise by some, disgust by others, again by ridicule, and awoke in some hopeful hearts the fond anticipation that the end of the Papacy was at hand. How did Brother Jonathan take it?"

"Pretty much in the same way. The press always put it in a ridiculous light, or drew from it 'confirmation strong as Holy Writ' that Pius IX would be the last Pope —that the definition was but a final and unavailing effort to prop his crumbling tiara," said I.

"It was a strange way to prop it," replied Maitland. "I don't quite see the connection."

"Nor I," I replied, "but that was the talk. It was a strange infatuation in the old man to attempt, in this 19th century, to cram such a far fetched absurdity down the throats of intelligent people."

"And yet he did 'cram it down,' as you say—stop for a moment and think—did a single Catholic leave the Church by reason of that definition?"

"I certainly did not hear of any, but—"

"And if there had been, even an ignorant servant girl, who protested against it, don't you think you would have heard of it? Some religious paper would have noticed it —some zealous minister, on the lookout for 'converts from Romanism,' would have eagerly seized the opportunity and spread the glad tidings far and wide."

"Yes, you are right. If there had been we would have heard of it. Well, what of that? It only goes to prove the admirable system pursued and established by the Catholic Church—like a well disciplined army marching as one man into the jaws of destruction at the voice of its leader."

"My dear fellow, it proves nothing of the kind; it proves that there was something in the dogma to satisfy human reason or it would not have been so universally accepted."

I looked up at him in surprise and a doubt if I understood him correctly.

"I beg your pardon," I said; "I judged from your first words on the subject that you were as far from Catholicity as I am; if you are a member of that Church I am sorry to have expressed myself so freely and will say no more."

Maitland laughed.

"Don't fear for my feelings, Mainwaring, I am no Catholic; indeed, you behold in me a candidate for orders in the Established Church, being, as you know, that unlucky individual, a third son. No, I am only taking a Catholic or Pickwickian view of the case. Take into consideration the Catholic's belief of the nature of Christ, and you must see that the Immaculate Conception of His Mother follows—'goes without saying,' as the parlez-vous have it. We Protestants view Christ's nature differently, accordingly as we individually interpret the New Testament. All of us deny with Nestorius the *consubstantiality* of the Son of God—some deny that He was God at all—others acknowledge that He is, in a manner, God—that the God-head was given to Him in His baptism, when the heavens opened and the dove descended—others that He was God from His birth but not *before*. Now the Catholic Church teaches that the God nature and the man nature were welded together, as it were, one and indivisible, from the *first moment* of His existence. Then, if this Child, born of Mary, was man, He took His flesh and blood from her—subject to the same penalties that hers was; but if He was God, also, before his birth, it follows that *God* could not come in contact with sin or with what had for ever so short a time been under the bann of sin. Therefore, God could not take flesh and blood from a sinful woman; she had to be pure 'from her conception' to be the *Mother of God*. Purity could not come from impurity, holiness from sin, and sin in the mother implies sin in the child in ordinary cases. Therefore, I say, to the Catholic's belief of or in the Divine nature of Christ, the Immaculate Conception follows as a necessity."

"Yes, as you put it, it does. But why did the Church, which makes such pretensions to honor the Mother of *God*, leave out, until the 19th century, the brightest jewel of her crown?" I asked.

"That is what I think, too, but you know they say it is not a *new* dogma; nothing is *new* in the Romish Church, if its defenders are to be believed. They claim that the Church has always held and taught that Mary was Immaculate, although it is only of late years that it has been deemed necessary to define positively what it behooves all good Papists, under pain of *anathema maranatha,* to believe on the subject."

I laughed.

"Upon my word, Maitland, you have it all as pat as any Romanist of them all; you speak as if you believed it."

"I might and no harm done."

"Why, what would your clerical superiors say?"

"There is no need for them to say anything or to know anything, if I choose to believe in the Immaculate Conception; there is nothing in the Thirty-nine articles to the contrary. I can swear to them with a clear conscience, and believe what I please. I was very much interested when the dogma was '*defined*,' and read all they had to say in favor of it, and, as I tell you, I think it the only logical conclusion a Catholic can come to."

"But, one moment; you say 'sin in the mother implies sin in the child,' therefore the mother of Mary must have been immaculate, also her mother before her, and so on back to David, who, my dear fellow, did not conform to the grace given him, if he had it!" said I.

"You leave out of mind the miraculous nature of the business; I spoke with reference to that; it was a miraculous favor bestowed upon Mary, and Mary alone—so the definition says."

"Why could not the 'miraculous favor' have been conferred on Christ Himself?"

"There comes your Protestantism again, with its human nature in Christ *apart* from the Divine. A Catholic does not admit that, therefore, there could be no favor conferred on Christ like that. He could require no such favor since there was no sin in Him. His man-nature was God, as much as His God-nature was man, they believe."

"Well, I confess never to have seriously thought upon the subject. To tell the whole truth, religion and Sabbath schools and the Sabbath were made such bugbears to me when a child by the puritanical spirit of my New England associations, that when I could I gladly threw aside all the trammels; and while I am not an irreligious man, I am no churchman. The only part of my early religious training which I retain is a dislike and abhorrence of Catholicity, and, in a measure, of Catholics. At the same time, I must acknowledge, to be candid and fair, that my prejudices always prevented me from making any inquiry into the truth or falsehood of their doctrines."

I suppose I spoke wearily, for I was feeling so, and Maitland, quickly noticing it, rose to go.

"I fear we have talked too long, old fellow, and you will have a bad night in consequence. We must be more careful in future, and I think it is likely we will have sufficient time to discuss this question and a few others during your convalescence. How is the arm?"

I replied that it burned and throbbed, and asked:

"How, in the name of common sense, did I fall so as to break it?"

"Don't ask me any particulars of that

interesting scene," he replied, laughing, " for I can give you none. I was only too glad to drag you out of the melée to notice any. But indeed you must get quiet, and now good night; to-morrow, if you choose, we can discuss the interesting subject at greater length in the daytime, when there will be no danger of destroying your night's rest. *Buona notte, dorme bene.*"

But there was no "*riposa bene*" for me. I was too nervous to rest. Our conversation had started a train of thoughts entirely new to me. I was not allowed to smoke, and so had no way of soothing myself into quiet and sleepiness. Sitting at the window where Maitland had left me, I mused upon many things.

Where were you at that moment? If you were still at Paris, doubtless, as it was Sunday, and you a careless seeker after pleasure, you were sipping *eau sucrée* in some boulevard restaurant, watching the gaily dressed *bourgeois* taking their weekly *divertissement.* I could not turn my eyes outward without their resting on the gleaming cross, and gradually all my thoughts began to cluster around that symbol so sacred in the eyes of a large number of my fellow-beings.

Not that they dwelt particularly upon its sacredness. I thought, it is true, of the reason why it had come to be used as I saw it there, and something of a wish rose within me that I could understand and feel a little of the faith that put it there. But I went over all which had been done in its name from the time of Constantine and his wondrous labarum, with its legend, that graceful mediaêval fable, to the days of Alva in the Netherlands and the Inquisition in Spain, and still further to the labors of a Marquette and a De Smet among our own Indians. And as I thought on all these things, Louis, the cross seemed to float in the blue ether, and I could almost imagine I saw the words glittering beneath it:

IN HOC SIGNO VINCES.

I sat a while longer and dwelt upon this

last fancy and then closed the shutters and drew down the blinds; but the idea was not so quickly shut out, and when I sought sleep it was with the words of the legend reiterating themselves in my mind with a persistency decidedly annoying. I tried to think of other things, and recited portions of several of my favorite authors. I counted from one to one million, but in vain; pre-eminent above all were the words:

IN HOC SIGNO VINCES.

CHAPTER III.

Still LONDON, Oct. 20th '67.

STILL in London, Louis *caro*, still a prisoner and still haunted by that cross. Maitland has just left me, and we've been talking of you. He asked me when I had heard from you—to which I was obliged to answer "not at all." And then I told him of our agreement not to correspond, and of our rendezvous appointed for March next.

"A queer arrangement, certainly. Did you expect some extraordinary experience to fall to each one's share in that time?" said he.

"Louis seemed to; you know his excitable, impressionable disposition. He seemed to regard us as knight-errants out in search of adventures—modern Don Quixotes, in fact," was my reply.

"I shall write myself and tell him of the mishap which befel you in defence of a modern Dulcinea del Toboso; he'll enjoy the account mightily," exclaimed Maitland.

"No! no; I particularly request you not to do any such thing; if I were in danger of death it would be different; but as it is, let the first arrangement stand," I cried.

"Well, I will try to amuse you during your enforced confinement," replied he, pleasantly; "I thought perhaps, under the circumstances, you would like to have Gwynne with you."

I did not tell him how I did long for you, amico—how I do every day and every hour. But I said something about not intruding upon Sir George much longer—then he interrupted me.

"Not a word of that, 'an thou lov'st me.' It was I who got you into the scrape, therefore it is I who must see you out of it, even if there were no more selfish motive. So you are my prisoner, sir, until that obstinate arm heals; and after that, if you forswear my company, I will be the loser. I cannot hope to rival Gwynne in your regards, but I hope for a place for myself."

I could only hold out my hand in silence in response to that.

"But why is the blind down so closely over that window?" he continued. "It is the pleasantest lookout."

I laughed and told him of my meditation upon the cross and how the idea had haunted me. It followed me even in my sleep, for I had a most mixed-up dream. I thought I was the "youth who bore 'mid snow and ice a banner with the strange device," etc., and was making the Alpine ascent, when my banner was changed into a cross, beneath the weight of which I fell, and as I did so the labarum appeared in the sky with its inevitable legend.

"What an imaginative youth you are!" he laughed. "My slumbers were not disturbed. But shall we take up another dogma of Romanism and discuss it, or shall we fall to and abuse the superstitions and errors of the Scarlet Woman?"

"Neither," I replied. "Tell me about yourself. You say you are intended for the

Church. How soon do you take orders?"

"*Cela dépend.* It is a family living, and has always been held by a member of the family until the last eighteen years. My uncle, who had the living, died, and I being too young then to be inducted, it was given *ad interim* to an old college friend of my father's. When I grew to the proper age, an old aunt having died and left me a nice little legacy, which, added to what my father allows me, made me comfortably off for a single man with no fondness for cards, dice, or horses, or greater luxuries, I concluded not to dispossess the old gentleman, to whom I am very much attached, and, my father being willing, to await his promotion or removal."

"Why not seek some other profession?" I asked.

"And break my father's heart!" he replied. "Why, man, he would be distressed beyond everything if I drew back from the arrangement. Maitland Rectory in the hands of strangers? As soon think of Maitland Grange passing away from the family!"

"Is that the only motive you have?"

"Pretty much. The life will suit me as well as any other; I doubt if I were Sir Alan at the Grange I would lead any very different one from what I will at the Rectory. As I said before, I have no very *wild* tastes, nor expensive ones, and can follow the hounds as well in a black coat as in a red one; play whist with the dowager guests at the Grange, and preach two sermons a day on Sunday, without very great self-denial. Of course my club must be given up and one or two other little things that suit a lay bachelor very well but would not harmonize with a clerical one."

He lay back in his lounging chair and patted his patent leather boots with his cane, while he pulled his whiskers meditatively. I took in the *tout ensemble* silently. He was so very unlike a man upon whom was soon to rest the serious responsibility of human souls, with his careless bonhommie and pleasure-loving nature, his little vanities of dress and person, and all the thousand and one triflings which one expects in a man of fashion, but would hardly be looked for in a minister of the gospel. Presently I spoke:

"You are reading, are you not, and preparing yourself for the life you intend to lead?"

"Not by any means; I shut up my books when I left college and shall have plenty of time to open them again when I am once established at the Rectory. As for preparation, I don't see that much of that is needed. Of course I shall cram for the examination, but that is a mere form. Lord —— knows my father and is a great friend of the bishop's, and they know that the living has always been in the family, so there will be no difficulty; besides, I don't need any whitewashing; my standing at college was good."

"Well, I suppose it is all right," I replied.

"Why, of course it is! Would you have me going about wearing hobnailed shoes and a long-tailed coat all these years? You see you Americans don't exactly understand the workings of our admirable Establishment. It is a great thing for younger sons, and I really don't see how we should manage without it. When you next come to England, I will very probably be settled and shall be most happy to see you at the Rectory."

"Thank you," I replied, laughing. "Who knows what may happen by the next time I visit England! But what is the news from Italy?"

"Oh, all goes serenely. The Garibaldians are slowly but surely approaching the gates of Rome, and, of course, as soon as they are near enough, the Roman people will rise to a man and bid them welcome, in spite of Pio Nono and his Frenchmen."

"I hope it may be so," I replied.

After sitting a few moments longer, he left me, saying:

"Here is the last from Mudie; so don't try Excelsior or Constantine again. *Au revoir.*"

But Mudie's volume was not opened. Neither did I dream of Constantine. But I did muse long and earnestly upon the conversation we had just had, and on the "admirable" workings of the system of the Established Church. And the result of my musings was the conclusion that as a means of supporting the younger members of noble or gentle families the system might be considered "admirable;" but as a Church, a guide to heaven for Christian souls, a source of comfort in affliction, of support in weakness, or strength in doubt, there was nothing tangible, nothing heaven-sent. And where would we find all those qualities, Louis, in the religions of the day? Suppose you and I, amico, should suddenly discover that we needed something more tangible than the *laissez aller* idea of religion which we now hold, where should we turn? Certainly not to the Church of England or the Episcopalianism of our own country—a religion of empty forms, of cold respectability; not to Presbyterianism or its offshoot Congregationalism, with its pharasaical sanctimoniousness and horrible doctrine of predestination; not to the shouting Methodist, taking a highly-wrought state of nervous excitement for a "conversion;" nor to a Baptist. Parkerism, nor Emersmianism, nor Swedenborgism meets the need. The Romanist will tell you it is in the one, holy, Catholic, &c., Church. But we'd have to go back a cycle or two for that—wouldn't we, Louis? —"become as little children," not only in credulity, but in ignorance and proneness to superstition, and close our eyes to all the progress the world has made in science and literature in the three hundred years since Luther tore the veil away that bound the people's eyes.

And this brings me back to the present. I am anxious about you, amico. If you are in Italy, for my sake, for your father's sake, above all for Eleanore's sake, keep out of the melée. I know your excitable nature, and I feel almost sure you will not be able to resist the magnetism of the old red-shirted hero if you are anywhere within his influence. I can preach to you, Louis, yet I could prove myself false to my own advice, and shoulder a musket in the good cause myself were not circumstances so strongly against it. As it is, I can only wish the glorious old man "God speed," and trust that he will at length succeed in his grand effort for the overthrow of priestly rule and Jesuitical tyranny in poor down-trodden Italy.

Well, I must bring this to a close. Here is nearly the first of November and my arm in a sling still, and nothing of my work done yet. But there is nothing for it but patience, and so I wait.

CHAPTER IV.

Still LONDON, Nov. 1, '67.

SINCE I closed my last letter, amico, matters have mended a little. I can leave my room, although my arm is still in a sling. To-day has been dull, dusty, and dark, threatening rain, and cold and dismal. Sir George and Lady Maitland left London last week, and we are expected to follow them the beginning of next. They are very kind and will not listen to my leaving them.

And now, Louis, old fellow, where in the world do you suppose I've been to-day?

"Teddy, my boy, what say you to visiting the church whose spire has haunted you so long, this morning, to hear what the clergyman will have to say on the dogma of the invocation of the saints? This, you know, is All Saints, and we could not have a better opportunity. If the Reverend gentleman whom I heard on a previous visit should be the preacher, you will have a treat, for he is an eloquent speaker and a really fine scholar," Maitland loquitur.

That's how I came to go, Louis, and it was a new experience for me, for you know I had never been inside of a Catholic church before nor witnessed any of their ceremonies.

We had very good seats near the pulpit, and at the proper time a clergyman entered it.

"We are in luck," whispered Maitland. "'Tis the one I heard before."

I glanced up at the preacher, and then looked again, for the pure, intellectual face that met my gaze, the soft, large eyes, the clear cut features, and the white, slender hands that rested on the edge of the pulpit, all irresistably attracted me. There was a rustling through the church for a few seconds as the congregation settled into an attentive attitude, and then silence unbroken by a sound.

"In the name of the Father, and of the Son, and of the Holy Ghost."

The voice was low, but every word distinct; the intonation so clear and pure that all in the large church heard without the slightest strain. I watched the hands as they made the sign of the cross with a sort of fascination.

Then the clergyman opened the Bible before him and read:

"Zachariah, 1 chap., 12 v.: The angel of the Lord answered, and said: O Lord of Hosts how long wilt Thou not have mercy on Jerusalem and on the cities of Judah, against which Thou hast had indignation these three score and ten years.

"Revelations, 5 chap., 8 v.: The four-and-twenty elders fell down before the Lamb, having every one of them harps and golden vials full of odors which are the prayers of the saints.

"Revelations, 8 chap., 3-4 v.: And another angel came and stood at the altar, having a golden censer; and there was given unto him much incense, that he should offer it with the prayers of all saints upon the golden altar which was before the Throne. And the smoke of the incense, *with the prayers of the saints,* ascended up before God out of the angel's hands."

Then he began his sermon, and I was much struck with the clear, logical arguments he used to support the doctrine of the invocation of saints. He explained that doctrine very fully and distinctly. I had always thought of it as a sort of idolatry, contemptuously and ignorantly condemning it. But, to be candid, I can do so no more. The true idea has something very beautiful in it. Then, in speaking of the veneration of the cross, he used the following words:

"And clothed with this sign the martyrs went forth, strong in their weakness, to conquer by their death; it was this holy symbol which led the virgins safe through the temptations of earth to their heavenly bridegroom; it was with the power of the cross that a Xavier converted the Indies, that a Loyola subjugated himself."

I watched the ceremonies of the Mass,

which followed, very closely, and though I could not fully understand them, I was struck by the solemnity. During the singing by the choir of the "Credo," I picked up a book which was lying in the pew, and opened it at the "Ordinary of the Mass." I found the prayers the priest was saying in Latin there, with an English translation on the same page. I read them through and thought them very appropriate, and find they are not "mummeries" by any means, but that each act and word has a signification which, to the Catholic, must be very beautiful. In fact I have had a "new revelation," a new set of ideas altogether, on the subject of Roman Catholicism. I should like to hear that preacher again, and told Maitland so, asking him if he knew him.

"No," replied M., "but if you wish to make his acquaintance, nothing is easier; these men are always approachable, it is their *rôle*, and his house joins the church."

Nov. 2d.—I was very much tempted to go over to the church to-day, and was very much in hopes Maitland would propose it, but he did not. I heard the church-bells ring, and saw the people crowding in, and in my heart, Louis, I longed to be able to believe as they did. Not *what* they did; but to believe something with the *certainty* of having the truth to rest on; not blown about by every wind of doctrine, as we, in our liberal ideas of religion, are; after all, a a certainty in such matters is very *restful*, and even a man's mind needs something besides itself to support it. We are not the self-sufficient creatures we would have the "weaker vessels" believe us to be.

I have you very much in my mind to-day. Is it ominous? Are you in danger or trouble? I can only hope not, and pray you may not be in any. For I have taken to prayers lately, *amico*, an observance I have neglected almost ever since I used to repeat my "Now I lay me down to sleep" at my mother's knee. I say "Our Father" every night before I retire—that I neglect it in the morning, I acknowledge; perhaps on the principle of the little boy, who, when asked if he said his morning prayers, thought any little boy could take care of himself in the daytime. An old story, but a very natural one.

And I have another confession to note down, Louis. I was passing a Catholic bookstore the other day, and seeing a prayer-book in the window, I was suddenly prompted to obtain and examine one. I did so. It is "Prayers of the Oratory," by Father Faber, and it has been a daily study. Of course, Maitland knows nothing of the purchase, and I take good care that he shall not.

Well, we leave to-morrow for the North, and my next letter will be dated from Scotia's romantic soil.

Good-bye, Louis, and God bless you, and may he grant that in this weary six months of unnecessary separation, we be not drifting apart for a lifetime.

CHAPTER V.

Aberdeen, Nov. 23d '67.

My Dear Louis:

 have been so busy, so hurried about from place to place, that I have not had time to jot down one of my "letters" to you, or for your benefit.

Sir George Maitland has been very kind, and has given me much genuine assistance in my business, and it is by his advice that I am here, after a couple of weeks spent very pleasantly at Maitland Grange, where I met the rest of Sir George's family: his oldest son, George, Henry, his second son, in the army, of course, and his daughter, Margaret, a "sonsie Scotch lassie," as genuine and true as the rest of them.

While there, I was not free from my mental restlessness or anxiety on the subject of religion, and one day, being by myself, I managed to pay a visit to the minister of the "kirk," in Peebles, near which town Maitlands is situated.

I told him, after a few "*façons de parler*," a *little* of the anxiety of mind from which I had been suffering.

"Ah!" exclaimed he, "you have at length discovered that you are a sinner, and would turn to Christ, and wish to know where to find Him. In the Bible, sir, in the Bible, and nowhere else."

"I doubt if you understand me, sir," I replied. "The Bible is well enough, but there is something wanting back of that. Christ did not write the Bible, it was not written until many years after Christ had died. Surely there was 'searching for Christ' in those earlier days. Where did they go to find Him?"

"To the Apostles, of course."

"Then the Apostles held the truth before the Bible was written?"

"Unquestionably?"

"And held it also after the Bible was written? The New Testament, I mean, of course?"

"Certainly, all those who were living."

"Then if they taught the truth, it was transmitted by them to those who came after them, and was taught by them independently of the Bible?"

"Certainly."

"Then why, when I come to you, do you send me to the Bible? I can read the Bible at home, and take all the comfort it can give me. But I want more, I want some authority that what I draw from the Bible is the truth, is the true interpretation of the Word."

"That you must find in your own inner consciousness. Search the Scriptures, and if in that search you find Christ, then know that your salvation is secure, and go on your way rejoicing; you have done all and can believe on Christ, and feel confident that you are one of the elect. But if you close that sacred volume without finding Christ, then there is no hope, for out of Christ there is no salvation."

"But I ask you, sir, how am I to know that I have found Christ?"

"Your own heart will tell you. You may be a long time finding him, the travail may be violent, your body may sink under it, but it will come at the end like a stroke of light. Christ will touch the troubled waters, and say, 'Peace, be still,' and in an instant your sins will fall from you like an old garment, and you will stand 'clothed in the sanctification of the Lord.'"

"Do you mean to say that this transformation will come by simply reading of the Scriptures?"

"By a prayerful reading of them, a prayerful reading."

"And suppose the cnange comes, what must I do to preserve it?"

"Nothing. You are then assured of your salvation, and may rest in Christ. You can do nothing of yourself to hinder or increase it."

"Even if I fall into the blackest sin, am I still sure of my salvation?"

"Even then. 'Though your sins be red as scarlet, I will make them white as snow,' are the words of the Bible. Even then, if you still believe in Christ you are safe; such is God's great mercy to sinful man."

Such was a portion of the conversation, Louis. I have given enough to convey an idea of it. And by this, you may imagine, I was not satisfied, by any means. The Reverend gentleman was very polite, and begged me to come again, after a prayerful reading of the Divine Word, and he would more fully explain to me the precious doctrine of election and predestination.

Need I tell you I did not go again. That visit was sufficient to show me that the Westminster Confession was not calculated to satisfy the cravings for something tangible, in the way of belief, which had arisen within me so suddenly and so inexplicably.

So I left Peebleshire without another visit to the "kirk," and, I dare say, the good man with a sigh has consigned me to the number of the lost.

Alan Maitland proposes to join me for a little Highland tour, which, cold as it is, I think I shall enjoy. And it is cold, my boy, I tell you!

CHAPTER VI.

Still ABERDEEN, Dec. 1st., '67.
AMICO MIO:

YOU see I am still stranded upon this far northwestern coast of Scotland. My business is progressing as nicely as I could desire, and I hope to be through by Christmas or the middle of January.

But Maitland cannot join me. The old Rector is dead. He was found dead in his study-chair by his wife, with his sermon for the next day half written before him. She had become anxious on account of his prolonged silence, and went in to see what was the matter.

The Rectory, therefore, being vacant, it behooves Alan Maitland to fill it as quickly as possible, and he is going, or has gone, down to Oxford, "to take orders," having a fondness for one of his old teachers there, and a fancy to receive his "Ordination" where he had pursued his studies.

"So," ended his letter to me, "when you get through your business in Aberdeen, and look in upon us as you go Londonward, I will be able to give you a welcome to the Rectory much sooner than I expected when we discussed the matter in town."

DEC. 5th.—I hope to get away from here by a few days before Christmas. I am perfectly well again, and thoroughly enjoy the cold, bracing air of this northern latitude; if only you were with me, Louis. Will we ever be together again as we have been?

AITLAND RECTORY, Dec. 24th.

I am again Maitland's guest, Louis, and Maitland unchanged and, I believe, unchangeable

Sir George and Lady M. are not at home, and Alan is to drive me over to Dalrymple Park, where they are staying, to-morrow. He met me at the station this afternoon with his dog-cart, and his first words were:

"Well, am I much changed by my new character?"

I replied that he was not, except that the straight coat and white cravat gave him an older look. Then, naturally, I asked him how it felt.

"Oh, all right. I suppose I'll get used to it in a little while. But you look thin and altered, what's the matter?"

This remark startled me. Has the mental conflict I have been going through indeed affected my personal appearance? I answered him lightly, that I had overworked myself, perhaps; that was all. To which he good-naturedly replied:

"Well, you must take a rest. I've got somebody to preach for me to-morrow, and I'll take you over to see the old folks, with whom, you know, you are a great favorite. They are staying at Dalrymple, just a pleasant ride from here, right in the heart of a country doubly interesting from its natural beauty, even in winter, and being the scenes of Scott's Waverly. In our immediate neighborhood we have the hut of the Black Dwarf, which you must also see. In addition to the natural and *Scottish* interest attaching to Dalrymple and its neighborhood, there are two or three beautiful and accomplished girls there," he said as we drove along.

"I've added a few comforts to the old house, but have changed nothing materially," he continued, as we drew up at the gate, and the groom came out to take the horse.

When we entered the house, I appreciated more fully the truth of his remarks. "A few comforts!" Why, Louis, even your luxury-loving nature would have been satisfied with the *few*. As I gazed round the drawing-room and "study," I inly pictured to myself the master of all this luxury called to "minister" to the dying wants of some poor peasant, whose chief idea of ease and happiness had been a "bit binnock," obtained without *killing* toil, and time to sit outside his cabin door and watch the sun go down upon a Sabbath evening. How could the rich man know and meet the poor man's needs, how sympathize with his sorrows, how understand him in the slightest way?

Dec. 27th.— As we drove over to Dalrymple on Christmas Day, I asked Maitland how he could reconcile it with his conscience to leave his flock—deserting them on his first Christmas as their pastor.

"I have not deserted them, my dear boy," he exclaimed. "I took the trouble to provide a substitute, what more can they ask? To tell you the truth, I was determined not to preach before you. I had not the courage."

To which I replied that I could not see what in me could alarm him, and added that he might have lost the opportunity of gaining a new member to his church, which he did not seem to think at all likely.

We had a delightful drive the twelve miles through the keen, frosty air, and were kindly welcomed at Dalrymple. On learning it was my intention to return to London the middle of the next week, Sir George and Lady Maitland both urged me to go at once to their house. They would not themselves be in town until February, when Parliament met, but she would write to the housekeeper to make me as comfortable as possible.

An invitation so kindly and sincerely given could not but be accepted in the same spirit. We returned here the next day, and to-morrow I take my departure. I think in another week I can write finally to my uncle of my success in bringing my business to a satisfactory conclusion.

I have had a very pleasant visit, and Maitland has devoted himself very thoroughly to my entertainment. He is a complete study to me and a puzzle. I cannot understand how he allows the responsibilities of his position to sit upon him so carelessly, how he reconciles his light-hearted bonhommie with the sacredness that is supposed to attach to his profession.

I do not like the Church of England, Louis, there is no consistency in it, not that I take the solitary instance of Maitland's carelessness as a criterion. I have been keeping my eyes about me, and wide open for the last two months, and I am convinced of the emptiness of its pretensions. To my mind it is but the work of a Parliament subservient to a sovereign's vices—the hand of God was not in its establishment. Whatever of good it has in it was borrowed or stolen from the old Faith which it superseded, then eliminated to such a degree that there is hardly a trace of it left. Those who sincerely build their hopes upon it, and trust to its guidance, are constantly feeling that they are leaning upon a reed which may break beneath their weight at any time. And those whose eager desire to find in it what they would like to find, drives them to test its utmost capacity for giving help, go so far on the road to Rome, that I wonder all don't follow Faber and Newman and go the rest of the way.

But I must say good-night. If I do get through, as I expect, next week, what shall I do with myself until the "meet" in March?

CHAPTER VII.

LONDON, Jan. 1st 1868.

HAPPY New Year, *amico*, to you, wherever you may be! A happy, happy New Year! I am once more in London, with my legal work well nigh completed, once more a guest of Sir George Maitland, and once more under the influence of that cross!

The trees are bare and allow me to see the white marble façade of the church, with its graceful spire, as well as the cross which crowns it.

And when I shall have finished my work, *amico*, what am I to do with myself? A thousand maledictions on the stupid arrangement we made on parting! If I knew where to find you I'd start right away and join you, but I might chase you over half the Continent and after all have to return to Cologne before I came up with you.

Jan. 6th.—My letter to my uncle to-day contained the last line of business which I will be obliged to write. The matter is arranged completely and satisfactorily; and now the question comes up again: What shall I do with myself? Go back to Maitland Rectory? No. Kind as Alan is, I take no satisfaction in watching the life he leads. I don't think we are congenial spirits.

I am not a recluse by any means here in London. Several friends of Alan's knowing of my being here have called upon me and invited me to their Clubs, their houses being shut up. I think I'll kill time during the next six weeks by studying "Club Life in London;" maybe I could write a book on it.

Jan. 26th.—I have allowed all this time to elapse since beginning this letter, Louis, because I could not write. I tried studying Club life, and found, as we say over the water, it *didn't pay*. Indeed, my mind is too much occupied by the train of thought which seems to have taken possession of it to allow of the intrusion of more trifling ideas, nor can the common-places of ordinary life change its bearing. I have followed the advice of the Presbyterian minister, and made the Bible a close study for the last three weeks, devoting every moment of my solitude to it. With what result?

A full conviction that all the talk of finding it the only rule of faith is nonsense and will not bear for one moment the test of a logical syllogism. There is always something back of the Bible—some authority pointing towards the Bible—with Presbyterians as well as with Episcopalians, only Presbyterians, having talked so very much of the Biblical rule of faith, think they really take it as such. Their *faith* is fixed and unwavering, not because they get it from the Bible, but because they do not.

For it stands to reason that he who regards the decisions of other men as mere human opinions, and therefore liable to be erroneous, must necessarily have the same idea of his own; how, then, can he find what he is required to believe unto salvation from the Bible alone without an inspired guide? Most assuredly he will find himself involved in perplexity, and totally unable to determine what to reject and what to receive. Therefore a man cannot safely take the Bible alone as a rule of faith, for it is one he cannot examine without being so firmly fixed in *some* faith that *nothing can* shake it.

And that is the fact. Protestant children receive religious instruction from their parents and pastors before they are able to judge for themselves. And when they are able, they take the Bible to find, not a new revelation, but confirmation of what they have already been taught. The Bible rule of faith amounts to this and nothing more. There is a hitch somewhere in the practical working of the system.

I have given the subject long and continued study, and find no rest to my mind or consolation for my troubled heart in Presbyterianism. Nor in the Established or Episcopal Church, as we call it. Can I find it in Methodism or the belief of the Anabaptist? I fear not; certainly I have no desire to seek it there, for I am satisfied I will not find it.

Yet, in the depth of my soul I feel the need of some decided religious belief. Our lives, *amico*, have been wonderfully pure considering the merely civilized pagans we have been. What has preserved us from contaminations that others deem matters of course? Was it not that, with all our carelessness, we *knew* there was something better than the lives we saw others lead, though we did not how to find it, just as through all the mummeries and superstitions of the Indian and Chinese there comes now and then a trace of the early labors of Christian missionaries in those countries before the blessed light had spread to Britain?

Is not this all that saves the godless world in this our day—the small remnant of Christianity, or, I should say, the latent leaven of Christianity upon which the modern structure of Liberalism and Progress is built?

76   IN SIX MONTHS; OR,

And what is the Idea of the Age but an effort to return to the Pagan civilization of anti-Christian Greece and Rome?—an effort defeated by the neglected but unforgotten teachings of a true religion.

FEB. 1st.—Another week of doubt and questionings, and, oh, *amico!* what a gulf yawns before me! Must I plunge into it before I will find rest of mind?

No, I will let the unfortunate matter drop here, take up the discarded threads of my old life and go on as before, letting all this study and thought be as naught. Yes, it comes to this: either I give up all idea of a religion or I become a Roman Catholic. Between the two there is no halting. I have studied Protestantism in all its phases, and I find its boasted "freedom of thought" is but the worst slavery to a human idea. Its promises are false, its doctrines can none of them be pushed to a logical conclusion without crumbling into a total denial of God, and its teachings are so contradictory that they can prove nothing. But, on the other hand, my intellect revolts from bowing with the servile abjectness of the Romanists to the teachings of their Church. If, on one side, the authority, or pretence of authority, is too weak, on the other it is too strong, asking too much, and I will not yield. This investigation has gone far enough, and it shall be dropped at this point. Suffice it that I shall never feel "called to unite" with any Protestant sect— *au reste c'est assai.*

FEB. 15th.—So I thought in my blind foolishness and pride. "*L'homme propose, mais le Dieu dispose.*" I could not throw the matter aside and resume my old life. That can never be again. I have fought, God knows how sturdily, against the conviction forced upon me that religious truth is only to be found in the Roman Catholic Church, but I was fighting against what "is mighty and shall prevail," and it has.

CHAPTER VIII.

LONDON, Feb. 2d, 1868.

MY DEAR UNCLE:

MY letters to you have not been satisfactory lately, I am aware, for the very good reason that I have not been satisfied with myself.

My dear uncle, my kind friend! I have a painful task before me to-night, a task from which I have shrunk for some weeks, and which ought to have been fulfilled sooner. And yet, now that I have set myself to the doing of it, it grows more painful. To you the confession I am about to make will sound like the blackest ingratitude, and how can I induce you to think it is not?

You know I am not a man of many words, but you also know that my affections are deeply rooted. You know, too, that, of all the world, you and Gwynne are my nearest and dearest. Therefore you will believe me when I tell you that, no matter how you may think proper to act after I have finished, whether you cast me off or still give me a place in your heart, my feelings towards you can never change—will rather become intensified.

With this case which I have just attended to for you I wish to close our business relations, thanking you for all you have done to forward my worldly prospects, and assuring you again of my unfailing and unalterable love and gratitude.

I shall not speedily return to the United States—never, unless it be in a far different character from that in which I left it. There are a few trifles of mine—a desk, some pictures, and books—left in my room, for the disposal of which I will send you directions in my next letter. For, whether you answer this or not, I shall write to you again to tell you of my final arrangements: they are so indefinite yet, it is not worth while to mention them.

And now to tell you, in as few words as

possible, what it is which has brought about this great change in all my plans for life:

I am about to become a Roman Catholic.

How this stupendous change was brought about I can hardly tell, it was so insidious and gradual. It began, I think, while I was confined to this very room last fall, recovering from the effects of my nocturnal adventure. It grew from the time I heard a sermon, on the first day of November, on the invocation of the saints, and has been growing ever since. To-morrow I mean to apply to the preacher of that day for advice and guidance.

You know you have often told me I was too prone to solemn and serious views of things, to morbid fancies, etc.; not that religion, or any one special form of religion, occupied my mind, but on general subjects of thought and feeling.

You will readily understand, then, how the question of the truth of Catholicity would force itself upon me when once brought to my mind by an accidental conversation during the many hours I was necessarily alone, and which I could not fill by constant reading, and writing and smoking being forbidden; also, when I was within hearing of the bells of a Catholic church three times a day, and literally under the shadow, or, I should say, under the benediction, of its cross.

The simple fact of being very ill would bring serious thoughts to my mind—questions as to why life was given to us and how it was best to carry out our Creator's will in our regard, and many others of like nature. That my thoughts turned to Catholicity was because of the above associations and circumstances.

After I went into Scotland the train of thought still clung to me, fight against it as I would, and that I did fight against it you will believe, knowing my prejudices previously.

I reviewed my old Puritan teachings, I consulted a minister of the Presbyterian Church, I studied Presbyterianism in all its forms, hoping to find satisfaction and rest.

But in vain: I could find no beauty in its tenets, no truth in what it professed to teach. I tried to admire the Established Church in vain. I soon saw through the emptiness of its professions—that it was a hollow cheat, a vain pageant, with nothing but the support of the State to uphold it, the most of its doctrines false, and those that were in a measure true, when pushed to their natural and logical conclusions, led unfailingly to the Catholic Church. For the Methodist or Baptist doctrines I felt no inclination. The various "isms" of our own New England, but various forms of infidelity under other names, were as mere chaff, not calculated to hold me for one moment. And so it was that I found myself face to face as it were with the old faith, which had stood the test of centuries and fought the world for eighteen hundred years. And when I stood thus face to face with Rome I paused: a horror came over me at the thought of giving my assent to her teachings. I could not do it. I thought of all I should lose—not only friendships, but the giving up of cherished plans and ideas; of retrograding as it were from the progress of the age in all that is held sacred to man in the present day. For such was my idea still of Catholicity—how far from the truth I know now.

Gradually every bulwark behind which I entrenched myself succumbed, and finally I was obliged to acknowledge myself vanquished. Hand in hand with my wish *not* to believe went my dread of what effect my believing would have upon you and Gwynne, and these fears and anxieties have caused me hours, days, weeks of suffering.

Thomas A'Kempis says: "It is an easy thing to despise human comfort when we have divine." I have proved the truth of those words in the hours when I have felt that I could cast my burden at my Saviour's feet and feel in his love all consolation for what I had lost. But I have also felt the truth of what the same author further says: "But it is much, very much, to be able to despise all comfort, both human and divine." It is much, and what I cannot yet do, for I have experienced the agony of soul which is felt by those who despair of salvation—a state of mind you cannot comprehend, and which no physical suffering can equal.

And now, uncle, whether your reply to this assures me of your unchanged feelings towards me, and that you regard my Catholicity as not a sufficient reason for banishing me from your affections, or whether the answer I dread comes in words or in a silence as significant, let me thank you heartfully and sincerely for all your kindness, patience, and interest, and, believe me, your name and Gwynne's will be ever first in my heart and in my prayers.

—— Square, Lond., Feb. 1st, 1868.

My Dear Alan:

What I have to tell you will no doubt astonish you—perhaps make you angry with what you will call my blind infatuation. If it does, I must bear with your displeasure as best I may; I shall regret it. but it cannot be helped.

I need not remind you of our conversation in this room upon the dogma of the Immaculate Conception, or of my dream of Excelsior and the labarum. My dear Alan, the dream is fulfilled; I mean to become a Catholic. Whether, after that act is consummated, I take upon me the livery of the soldier of the Cross or try to save my soul amid the temptations of the world, I have not decided. As you, my dear fellow, were, in a manner, instrumental in the fact of my conversion, I shall ever cherish for you a warm and sincere friendship, whether you will value it or not.

Having just written a long letter to my uncle, and having still another one to write, I will close here, hoping to hear from you.

To-morrow I shall seek out the clergyman whom we heard preach that first of November and put myself into his hands.

LONDON, Feb. 1st, 1868.

CARO AMICO:

Although you will not read these lines

until you will have seen me and heard my story from my own lips, I cannot refrain from writing to you to-night, for it is the last night of my old life, amico, and perhaps the last in reality of our friendship.

I have longed so much to see you, Louis, during the last months, longed every day, and wearied for the grasp of your hand—the sound of your voice.

And now that the time for our meeting will soon be upon us, do you look forward to it as I do, with dread and apprehension?

But of course you do not; why should you?

I have fought against the dread of your displeasure, and tried to think I could bear that as I bear other things; but, old friend, the ties that bind our hearts together are too strong to be broken without pain. How little I thought when I urged you to cross the ocean with me what the result was to be —that we might never more visit the old familiar scenes together with the same love.

Shall what I have to tell you when we

meet change your feelings towards me? Will my words break up all the bonds which affection, association, memories of old times, dangers passed and perils encountered together, and all that goes to make up the meaning of the word "friendship" have drawn around us?

I hope not. Still, if it must, it must.

I have written to my uncle to-night, telling him of the change I contemplate. He is my only relative, and the pain I know my letter will give him is a cause of great sorrow to me. But that is nothing to the feeling of utter isolation which comes over me when I think of the past and look forward to the future.

I feel as if I stood alone in the wide world, with none to whom I could turn for help or comfort, just when I find what a poor, weak mortal I am and how I need them both.

But if they are denied me by my friends here, there is a source to which I can turn and which will never fail me. He who has withdrawn all worldly consolation will, I trust, presently fill my soul with a flood of heavenly joy and peace which nothing earthly can ever take away.

Think of me pityingly, then, oh! amico, and blame me not too severely when, after my confession is made to you, and you have read these lines, we part forever.

In a few weeks it will be decided, and this fever of dread and impatience, which is consuming me, over its fiercest burnin

CHAPTER IX.

LONDON, Feb. 2nd.

I STILL continue my journalistic letters to you, amico, because I cannot bring myself to resign a custom which seems to draw me nearer to you for a little while each day.

I wrote to you last night in great mental trouble, to which has succeeded a great and exceeding peace.

This morning, true to my resolution, I sought the clergyman whose sermon had so impressed me. But before I did so, I had a long and fierce struggle with myself. I paced my room until I was physically exhausted, and still the strife went on. The letters I had written the night before were yet upon the table; the act was not consummated; there was yet time to draw back and neither my uncle nor Alan Maitland need know anything about it; things would go on as they had been—there would be no change.

Would there not? The question forced itself upon me. I might conceal the fact of my mental struggles for the last three months from my friends, but could I forget them myself? could I do away with their effects upon my inner being? I might tell myself that I had begun the subject in a morbid, unnatural state of mind, and that as soon as I saw you and began the journey we had planned together my old feelings would return, and I would remember the sufferings of the winter as only the consequences of the feverish state I was in.

But was it so?

Twice I took up the letter to my uncle and was about to tear it—twice I laid it down; the last time, as I did so, the clear-toned bell from the church across the square rang out the Angelus, and as I glanced through the window my eye rested on the gleaming cross with the sunshine on it.

I hesitated no longer, but seizing my hat

and picking up the letters to put into the box as I passed through the hall, started on the visit.

I found the clergyman whom I sought (I had heard him preach again since my return to London and had then enquired his name) at home, and sending up my card awaited with nervous dread his coming.

But all unpleasant feeling passed as soon as Mr. Baine entered the room; there was such an expression of kindness, gentleness and true Christian charity upon his noble features, so much earnestness and strength in the expression of his beautiful eyes, that I felt I was in the presence of no ordinary man. He was also a polished gentleman, and his greeting to me was full of suavity and grace. After a few preliminary sentences, with a seeming intuition of what had brought me, Mr. Baine led the conversation into such a channel that I had no difficulty in opening my business to him without the least awkwardness.

At first I hesitated and spoke slowly, but

gradually (and Mr. Baine did not interrupt me by words, though he showed by his strict attention that he followed me closely) I grew excited as I gave words to the thoughts that had been at work within me, and surely the Reverend gentleman could see that my sufferings had been great.

"And now, sir," I concluded, "I have come to you to help me; I have tried to help myself and cannot. I have fought against the convictions that have been growing upon me; I have tried to satisfy myself with husks because I dreaded to stretch forth my hands for the fruit. I have studied the teachings of the Church of England and have gone back to my childhood's remembrance of Puritanism and Presbyterianism, but they do not satisfy my cravings. I ask them for bread and they give me a stone; I thirst and they lead me to broken cisterns in which there is no water. Can you give me the bread of life, by eating which I shall never hunger? Show me the fount of living waters springing to everlasting life. Tell me that you can, that you will; for if I cannot find what I seek *here*, having failed *there*, where shall I go—what shall I do?"

As I finished, I dropped my head upon my folded arms which rested on the table. Mr. Baine must have been much moved, for he did not speak for some seconds; then I felt a gentle touch upon my bowed head:

"'I am the Way, the Truth and the Life. No man can come to Me except the Father, who hath sent Me, draw him. Come unto Me all ye who labor and are heavy ladened and I will refresh you. I am the Shepherd, and My sheep know My voice; other sheep I have which are not of this fold, them, also, will I bring, that there may be one Fold and one Shepherd.' Let our Saviour's own words comfort you, my son, and may He grant me power to set your soul at rest."

Then he spoke to me words of comfort and consolation filled with the Spirit of his Divine Master. He did not repeat set phrases of cant, nor send me to the Bible without an idea of what I was to do with what I found there. But while he had a text ready in support of every argument, and his whole conversation showed a perfect and comprehensive familiarity with the Holy Scriptures, I found here what I wanted—the power behind the throne, if I may use the term; the authority which would be a guide and direction in the use of the Word of God—the Church, which had been made the custodian and expounder of His Word.

After an hour had sped so rapidly I hardly thought I had been with him fifteen minutes, Mr. Baine told me he had an engagement of obligation to fulfil, and kindly gave me my congè, telling me he would gladly devote several hours each day to me either here or at his own house.

As we proceeded towards the front door, he said:

"You probably do not know that this is the Feast of the Purification of the Blessed Virgin, kept in commemoration of her exceeding great humility, inasmuch as she, being the Mother of God and free from all taint of original sin, was above all law, yet she did not neglect to fulfil every tittle of the Jewish regulations, and without a word of question presented herself with the two turtle doves in the temple to be purified after the birth of her Divine Child. Our Lady must have some particular intention with regard to you, since it was a cross on a church dedicated to her Immaculate Conception which first drew your thoughts toward Catholicity, and you make the first step towards embracing the faith upon this beautiful festival. We have a chapel in the house dedicated to our Lady, where, upon occasion, the Blessed Sacrament is kept. Let us seek her there and place ourselves under her protection, asking her to lead you to her Son."

I followed him to a beautiful little chapel, the walls of which were painted blue, and the decorations of the little altar were all in the traditional colors of the Mother of God.

Over the altar hung a painting, a copy of Raphael's unsurpassable Sixtine Madonna.

Here we knelt in heartfelt prayer for ten or fifteen minutes, then I took leave of my kind friend.

CHAPTER X.

London, Feb. 27, 1868.

I HAVE not chronicled the daily events and doings of the last four weeks because I could not. The struggle through which I have gone has been so fierce, I had strength for nothing else. I wrote to you, amico, and to my uncle, that I had found the truth and meant to embrace it; yet, when it came to the point, the gift of faith seemed withheld. Much as I wished for rest from the anxiety which was so wearying, confident as I felt that rest was only to be found in the Church, I could not yield at once to the priest's arguments, but fought my way step by step.

Somewhere about the middle of the month I received the letter which I copy from Maitland:

"Quem Deus vult perdere prius dementat!"
You have been too much alone among strangers

this winter, and your brain is suffering from the effects. You say you have finished your law business. Then pack up and hunt out Gwynne without waiting to join him at Cologne, or, if you will not do that, come back here and see if I cannot exorcise the evil.

There is a gay party at the Grange, and several young ladies, charming in every respect—well born, handsome, rich. So you do not interfere with *my own* peculiar aim, you may draw a bead upon any of the others.

Therefore, pack up and come down, and let us hear no more of such morbid fancies as your last contained. Sir George wishes me to say to you that he will not be in London as soon as he first expected, and you are to continue to make yourself as comfortable as you can, unless you will accept my invitation.

You had better think well on it. My bachelor establishment at the Rectory is perfect, and you ought to avail yourself of it while it lasts; how long that will be, I can't say. Of course it is the proper thing for me to marry. A clergyman, like a doctor, is never half as successful single as when he has a better-half to *finesse*. Therefore, I am thinking of the matter, and I dare say I shall soon make my election. I hope that last letter was only occasioned by a fit of the blues and when you write next " Richard will be himself again."

I have written to-night to tell him that "Richard *is* himself again," though, I hope, a "wiser and a better" self. The struggle is over and the battle won. The ship that has been tossing so long upon the waves of doubt and uncertainty is safely moored in a sure harbor. I *am* a Catholic. Only this morning was the happiness conferred upon me. Mr. Baine has been very patient and very kind. He began at the very beginning, like teaching me my A B C again, and after proving to me the necessity to man's nature of some *revealed religion,* took me on up the steps of proof that the Roman Catholic is the only one which can claim that title, and the only one which can suit and meet our spiritual needs. He showed me the falsehoods upon which all others are built, how they had their origin in either the evil passions of a king, or the fanaticism of some self-worshiping enthusiast, or the wicked ambition of some proud monk, false to his vows and his better instincts.

I see now that the "Progress" they prate

so much about is but license; that there can be no true *progress* but in submission to God and an earnest desire to know His will and do it. I have found the meaning of the text: "Unless ye become as little children ye shall not enter the kingdom of heaven." It does not call for a blind slavery, unbecoming and unworthy of a man. It means that the proudest among us is, and must feel that he is, but a speck in the great infinity of the Almighty—but the breath of His nostrils; and it is only until he can and does feel this and bows himself at God's footstool in humble acknowledgment of the truth that he can begin to walk in the path of salvation.

The time of our meeting draws so near, Louis, that I will put pen to paper no more. I pray, my friend, that our love be not a thing of the past after that eventful day. I can answer for myself, amico, that always, as now, you will hold, of mortals, the first place in my heart, your name be the first in my prayers.

I have had a kind, loving letter from my

uncle and his wife. It has cheered me very much. They are grieved, troubled exceedingly at my "perversion," as they call it, but it will make to them no difference of feeling. My uncle wishes me to return and pay them a visit before I decide upon my future plans. I shall do so, Louis, and now it remains with you whether we return to the United States as we left it—together, or alone. And in a few days I shall know.

COLOGNE, March 5th.—Your letter instead of yourself greets me here, amico. What is the matter? I am most anxious, and start to-night for Sicily, through Italy, as fast as steam can carry me.

PART THIRD.

CHAPTER I.

LOUIS GWYNNE'S JOURNAL.

PARIS, Sept. 10th, 1867.

SPENT yesterday trying to get some of the vile English fog out of my lungs by remaining most of the time in the open air. And what a lovely day it was! And what a perfect city Paris is!

Everything is improved even in the short three years since I was here last. Certainly good Americans ought to be forgiven for mistaking Paris for Paradise, and France owes the Sphinx of the Tuilleries a great deal, if he does rule her with an iron hand.

The talk here is very much of Italian affairs, and the sympathizers with the revolutionists are full of hope that now, the Pope having lost his French supporters, Rome will become part of Italy. As a free citizen of a free republic, I suppose I ought to sympathize with the Italian people in their cry for freedom, and as a Protestant, I ought to hate the Pope and rejoice in the downfall of the Papacy, which is almost, in the opinion of many, *un fait accompli.*

But with all my glorious prerogative of freedom, and with all my Protestantism, I cannot help thinking there may be another side to the story.

Some of the Pope's subjects may be dissatisfied with his government, which, doubtless, shares the lot of all other governments and is not perfect (though, to my thinking, from Pius to Victor Emmanuel would be flying from "ills they have to others they know not of." However, I can say, with Virgil, "Tros, Tyruisve, mihi nullo discrimine agetur"), but the Pope has his rights as a sovereign as well as Victoria, and by all odds a stronger, because a longer claim to the purple; therefore, in my opinion, he was no more wrong in putting down rebellion than we were.

Perhaps I would take the talks of the clubs and papers for the truth and rant with the ranters if England had not, as she has always where disorder and rebellion are rife, "a finger," if not a whole hand, "in the pie," to use a vulgar but very pertinent saying. What England does, that do not *I*, and what England wishes I would prevent her accomplishing if I could.

As soon as it grows cooler, I think I shall go to Rome and see the thing out; be "in at the death," if there is to be a death; at any rate be on the spot.

SEPT. 12th.—My promise to Ed. to keep a journal is a bore; but a promise is a promise; he would be disappointed if I did not.

SEPT. 14th.—It is getting quite cool, and my inclination turns more and more Romewards. Next week I'll go, if nothing occurs to prevent.

I have been haunted all day by a voice. Yesterday, in the Louvre gallery,

a lady and gentleman, evidently father and
daughter, passed close behind me: the lady
was speaking—and such a voice! They
passed without pausing, and her head was
turned towards her companion and away
from me, but her figure struck me as extremely graceful and perfect, for all it was
so small, and the gentleman I saw distinctly.

SEPT. 15th.—How shall I describe her?
What words can sufficiently portray her
loveliness?

Last night there was a reception at the
Austrian ambassador's. I, with Paul de
Lessac, was standing near the door of the
entrance, when the usher announced:

"Monsieur le Comte et Mademoiselle
Manzano!"

I turned to look.

She was just entering, on her father's arm,
and stood in the doorway as in a frame, the
loveliest picture the human eye ever gazed
upon. She is an Italian blonde, that most
perfect of all created perfections. *Petite* in

figure, yet so exquisitely formed as to cause no wish for added inches to arise in the gazer's mind, the small head set perfectly on the slender throat and fine bust, was carried with a regal grace Eugenie might have copied. If in the curve of the delicate lips and chin and in the bearing of the beautiful head with its masses of golden hair there was aught of pride, the large eyes, when raised, were melting in their tenderness, and their appealing sweetness made all amends. At first those eyes would have been thought black; it was not until a nearer look revealed to me that they were blue that I was undeceived. But such a blue! Sea nor sky ever glowed with such a hue!

De Lessac started forward to speak to her, after the Austrian ambassador had welcomed her, and as she answered him, I recognized the voice; the old gentleman, her companion, I had already recognized, but I could not be sure it was she. Obeying an impulse I could not account for, I put as much space between us as I could, and presently found myself looking over a portfolio of photographs and engravings in one corner of the farthest room of the suite. Although my eyes were on the pictures, I saw them not, but I did see de Lessac's start when he found I had vanished, and the searching glance he sent around the room. Then he perceived me and made his way towards my corner with a good-natured smile:

"Ah, mon ami!" he exclaimed, "saw you ever anything more lovely? Are you not lost heart and soul? No one could blame you if you were."

But I could not join in the Frenchman's rhapsodies. To my excited senses, they seemed like profanity. So I asked quietly:

"How long has she been in Paris?"

"For some time. Next week, however, they return to Rome. Warm as it still is, they are both most anxious to get back, in view of this threatening of the Garibaldians. They are devoted heart and soul to the Pope. But, come, let me present you."

A thrill passed through me as he spoke. They were going to Rome next week; why should I not go too and in their company? Yet, when de Lessac put his arm through mine, I again shrank back.

"No, no!" said I, "pray excuse me, Paul; I prefer to worship at a distance for a little while; later in the evening I will be at your service."

Paul looked at me and gave one of those inimitable French shrugs of his, saying·

"Eh bien! You always were a queer fellow, Gwynne, mon ami, and if it were anyone else I should be really offended."

I felt that I had not reciprocated as I should to his kind offer, and raised my head to say as much, when I saw an old officer with a star or two on his breast go up to la Contessina and evidently make a request.

She replied by a gesture of assent and held out her hand, which the old gentleman raised to his lips before he laid it on his arm, and led her in the direction of the corner in which I stood.

On one side of me a door opened into the music room; on the other, the window gave upon a balcony without. Before they had time to observe me, I had stepped out upon the balcony, when I found, to my delight, a window similar to the one by which I had escaped opened upon it from the music room also. I could see and hear unobserved. Several of the company followed her into the room and more grouped themselves at the door.

Outside, the air was balmy and mild, and the harvest moon in full splendor; the gardens around the house subdued the noise from the street, and, in fact, the situation could not have been improved.

As la Contessina ran her fingers over the keys of the piano she showed herself a perfect mistress of the instrument. She played a brilliant prelude, then modulated into some minor chords and finally began the accompaniment. She sang with exquisite pathos the "O! mia Fernando!" in a voice of great natural sweetness and power, which had been studiously cultivated. I feared she would cease after one song, but no—she sang again, this time the "Casta Diva."

When she had finished, they gathered around her and showered praise and compliments upon her while I gazed up at the "Goddess chaste," rocking the last tones in my heart.

At last, as if tired of the flattery poured upon her, she struck the keys again, and there was silence. Then she sang "Avec les larmes dans sa voix," some simple German words to an air of Mendelssohn's; the melody sobbed and wailed through the minor keys with a plaintive supplication in the tones, which had such an effect upon me that I bowed my head upon the railing and sobbed aloud.

It was well I was alone.

After that song she wandered over the chords for a little while and then dashed off one of Chopin's mazourkas,—wild, giddy, fascinating in its weird beauty, and as she struck the last notes she rose from the instrument.

An hour afterwards I sought de Lessac and signified my desire to be presented; he was just a thought cool when I spoke, but I expressed my regret for any offense I might have given so sincerely, that his good nature would not permit him to retain the feeling.

"Don't be alarmed, Contessina, at my friend's English name; he comes from the far side of the ocean, not from across the Channel," said de Lessac, after the introduction.

Though her manner had been polite before she was reserved and cold; as soon as he spoke her eyes lighted up and she held out her hand.

"An American! Ah! I am glad you are not an Englishman; but, maybe, you come from Canada, and that—that is just as bad," she added, archly.

"I am happy, Contessina," I replied, bowing over the hand I held, "to proclaim myself a citizen of the United States, owing neither love nor loyalty to England."

"Ah! c'est bien! then we shall be friends, for I do not like England—she is—oh—je ne sais quoi."

"I know what she is," I replied, "but let us, for the present, consign her to the limbo she so well deserves, and 'seek no more her follies to disclose.'"

"Ah! I have read that poem—it is perfect! But I am willing to forget England for the present. We agree, then, do we, on other points?—I am a Catholic, Monsieur."

"There we differ, Contessina." Though at that moment I felt that I would be one for one smile of hers.

"Cela *n'est pas* bien!" she exclaimed, laughing, "and I don't know how you Protestant Americans can be excluded from my censure—you echo all England says about affairs in Italy! Of course you are a great admirer of that *misérable* Garibaldi?"

"I was, Contessina, I must confess, at first, deep in my admiration of a man who had nerve enough to raise his voice against what I supposed to be a most terrible tyranny, led to feel such admiration by my sympathy for every people struggling against oppression."

"But you don't know—you—"

"Pardon, Mademoiselle, I must interrupt you lest you misjudge me. By degrees my opinions changed, and changed entirely by watching and judging the character of the man."

"Ah! go on!"

"He is simply a fanatical demagogue, led on by hatred of everything good, fondness for notoriety, and love of English gold."

"Ah! that is true!"

"If I really thought he led the Italian people against a despotism which destroyed their rights as a people, I should bid him 'God-speed!' But, while I acknowledge the truth of your reproach that we Americans echo England in our opinions upon Continental affairs, and receive any falsehoods she sends us as truth, there are many among us who read and judge for ourselves. I have for a long time seen and felt that the 'Italian movement' would never have been but for English gold and English impudence, and Garibaldi, whether knowingly or not, is but the tool and catspaw of England."

"Bravo! Signor Gwynne, bravissimo!" she exclaimed gleefully, clapping her little hands. "Come to Italy and I will show you how much this 'Italian movement' has any real hold among the people, how they hate Victor Emmanuel and love our Holy Father, and, oh! then, then you will pray as I do that his enemies may be crushed and the last days of the grand old man be spent in a glorious peace!"

If I thought her lovely before, it was because I had not seen her in her present excitement; her eyes sparkled, and her cheeks glowed with a rich color, and her delicate lips trembled in the excess of her emotion.

"I am on my way to Italy, Contessina, and expect to start in a short time."

"We go next week, Mr. Gwynne. Can you not join us?" asked the Count, smiling upon his daughter's excited face.

I expressed my thanks, while my heart was in a tumult of delight, and in a few moments my new friends withdrew, after giving me their address.

I left the Legation and returned to my hotel as soon as she was gone, but sleep, gentle sleep came not to my eyelids, nor, indeed, did I woo her; my mind was in a tumult of thoughts, fancies, dreams, hopes, and wishes.

CHAPTER II.

SEPTEMBER 16th.

SPENT a delightful evening with la Contessina; we talked and sang, and tried over duetts, she asked me if I played any instrument, and when I acknowledged that I had a flute at my rooms, she would not be satisfied until she had sent a servant with a note to Jacques, my *valet-de-place*, telling him to send the instrument by the bearer. Then we had two or three hours of charming musical intercourse.

SEPT. 23d.—From Nice to Genoa, a day's boating along the shore nearly the whole way, and such a shore!

The Maritine Alps rise from the very edge of the Mediterranean, and tower peak on peak up, until their summits really seem to pierce the sky. Here and there, as the boat glided along, we could see the white walls of some villa gleaming among the trees, or the spire of some wayside chapel lifting the cross to heaven.

We remain all night here, but there are stronger attractions to keep me at the hotel than those of Genoa, *la Superba*, to draw me away, so I have seen nothing of the city during this visit; some years ago I explored its haunts and beauties thoroughly.

To-morrow by rail to Florence; thence we expect to experience some difficulty, notwithstanding the pretended innocence of complicity with the present movement assumed by the Italian Government, in reaching Rome. However, Count Manzano has friends at court, and may find them useful; as for me, "*quo me cunque rapit tempestas deferor hospes,*" as old Horace says, as long as it does not deprive me of the company of la Contessina.

This evening we sat out upon the balcony in the balmy air, and gradually the conversation fell into the old train, upon the, to her, absorbing topic of Pius IX and his difficulties.

According to her, the Pope is a saint ready for translation to the realms of bliss, and his enemies—spirits ripe for the fire which burneth but consumeth not for all eternity. *If there is such a fire!*

While I draw her out in this, her favorite subject, in order to enjoy the sound of her soft, sweet voice, and for an excuse to gaze upon her beauty—in short, as a reason for being beside her constantly—I cannot help being struck by the reasonableness of much that she says, and the strength of many of the arguments she uses, particularly when her father, with his calm, good sense and dispassionate logic, comes to her assistance, and checks, while he sustains, her overflowing enthusiasm.

This evening we were alone, and I could not help teazing her a little about the intolerance of Catholics, and their claiming for themselves all truth and true religion.

"But you mistake, Signor, you mistake;

we believe that many will be saved *malgré* their Protestantism; but surely we may be forgiven if, in looking around at the result of that Protestantism, we cling to our time-hallowed Church only the stronger!"

I wish I could fix upon this paper, Ed., the play of her lovely features, and fire of her beautiful eyes, but I cannot; nor can I follow her in her rapid enunciation, word for word, I can only give you the sum and substance of what she said. She speaks English idiomatically, but correctly; too slowly, however, for her thoughts. Consequently, she soon glides into French or Italian. The Count speaks English quite well, having, before his marriage, spent several years in that country, and visited it several times since.

She expressed herself utterly unable to see any beauty or worship in the cold formalities of the Protestant form of religious services. To her, the preacher seemed to care more for the manner than the matter of his sermon, and as for the rest of the service,

what was it? where was the soul of it?
What did it mean? Where is the Church
beside the Roman Catholic that speaks *ex
cathedra*, that dares to take a stand above
man's finite reason, and say to it, "you must
bend to me, not I to you?" What are the
teachings of the different sects? Are they
the same year in and year out? In fact, *do
they teach anything?* And supposing they
attempt to teach, is it not a mere attempt?
no reliance can be placed upon their teachings, one contradicting the other. Is not
all Protestantism a direct and clearly spoken
negation of everything but what *each individual chooses to believe?* They are like
Pilate, asking, what is truth, and going out
without waiting for the answer.

A Catholic cannot understand this as
religion.

Our religion takes our souls into its guar-
dianship from the time we can speak (before,
in fact, in the promises of our sponsors in
baptism), she lights the way to our darkened eyes, by her clear, steady radiance,

through childhood to youth, showing us how, when we have fallen, we can regain the ground lost; strengthening us when we are weak, and counselling us when we doubt, with a hand ever pointing out to us the goal of all our hopes; the reward of all our efforts; the rest for all our weariness; following us, nay, assisting and supporting us, even into the presence of our Judge; praying for us, working for us when prayers and works of ours avail no longer for ourselves.

And how does she do this?

By a set of formal prayers, and a sermon on Sundays?

Or the arguments of a man clothed in no religious authority, who sometimes does not believe what, as a receiver of a handsome salary, he is bound to please his hearers by preaching?

No! But by virtue of her truth, in teaching what Christ taught; by virtue of her *consistency*, teaching the same truths always and in all places; by virtue of His promise to be with her all days, instructing her in all things by the Holy Spirit. By virtue of her beautiful adaptability to all the wants of the human soul. Because she is perfect among imperfections; strong in the midst of weakness; holy in a world of sin. Because by all this she carries conviction to the hearts, and satisfaction to the minds of men.

And this religion, by its very essence, requires a *visible* head upon earth to direct and govern, a centre round which she revolves; a Rock to which, in a sea of doubt and fear, she can cling, and know that there the gates of hell cannot prevail. This head is the Pope, and every Catholic will defend the Pope through weal or woe.

"But," I asked, "is it necessary that this Head should be a temporal prince? Remember, Christ said, 'The foxes have holes, and the birds of the air nests, but the Son of Man has not whereon to lay his head.' Peter was but a poor fisherman, and when he went about his Master's work took neither staff nor purse."

"Yes, yes; I know that is the unfailing argument; hydra-headed—how often has it not been answered, but to spring up again! Our Saviour gave us an example of despising the things of this world, its pomp and glory, and forbade us to devote ourselves to them, but He did not forbid us to use them. On the contrary, He conformed in every way to the usages of the world and 'society,' if I may use the term, as it then was. Remember His rebuke to Peter; the feeding of the multitude in the desert, the tribute money in the fish's mouth.

"And as there must of necessity be a visible head to the Church of God, so that head must of necessity be trammelled by no allegiance to earthly potentate. As he is raised above them all by the supernatural position he holds as Christ's vice-gerent, so he must be independent of, or above them, in human government, in order that his first and most important office be not interfered with. *Cela va sans dire!* Is it not of necessity, that if the Pope resided either in France or Austria, the Emperor would wish to control his decisions, or there would be perpetual wrangling?

"But, you know," she continued, laughing, and blushing at her own warmth, "you acknowledge the injustice of attempting to deprive the Holy Father of his dominions on simply natural rules. You are only wishing to make me talk; so, one word more, and I have done. The Garibaldians may work and intrigue, Protestant nations and some unworthy Catholics may wish them to succeed, and give them substantial help, *it will be in vain!* They may prevail for a time, seemingly, it will be only for a time; Heaven battles on our side, and we shall conquer. The Pope is Rome's, and Rome is the Pope's, and shall be as long as time lasts!"

"*Ah, figlia mia, figlia mia!*"

She started, and turned to find her father standing behind her; he had come up unobserved and overheard her last remarks.

"My daughter, Mr. Gwynne," he said,

turning to me, "reasons, woman-like, from her heart, rather than her head; therefore, I pray you judge her not too strictly by logical rules. I sincerely believe that this Garibaldian movement will be unsuccessful, and hope and pray it may—but," and he raised his hat as he spoke, "we are in God's hands for weal or woe, and He only knows the end. It may please Him to humiliate the Church through her Head; it may be according to the designs of His Divine Providence that our Holy Father shall lose his temporal possessions; if it is so, He will so ordain matters that the Church shall not suffer in spiritual things: there, we have His promise to be with her all days.

SEPT. 24th. Florence. We start to-morrow for Rome. By Count Manzano's influence at court, and my own at the United States legation, we have had no difficulty in arranging our departure, and though the country is very much disturbed by Garibaldi's marauding bands, the railroad is guarded by the Italian troops as far as the Papal frontier.

Poor little Eleanore! I have had a letter of hers unanswered for two weeks! It is the first time in my life that I ever neglected the child, and hope she will forgive me after the letter I write to-night. She expected me to come to her direct from Paris, according to my first arrangement, and my not doing so was a great disappointment. I have spoken to la Contessina about Nellie, and she has made me promise to bring her to Rome this winter.

Later. I have just bade my friends good night, and left la Contessina in an ecstacy. Her father brought her the news, while I was there, of Garibaldi's arrest by the Italian government, near Sienna, as he was on his way to join his son, Menotti, who is advancing on Rome from the Neapolitan frontier.

I asked the Count if he thought the action of the Italian Government was a sincere one, with a desire to put an end to the trouble?

But he shook his head, and said he feared not. His hope was that Louis Napoleon would, notwithstanding this, send troops to Civita Vecchia. However, her father's anxiety did not affect la Contessina's delight at the news.

Well! To-morrow to Rome!

It is with very strange feelings that I approach, for the first time, the "Niobe of Nations." When last in Europe I had no time to go there, feeling that a mere cursory glance at the city, which was all a couple of weeks would give me, and I could spare no more to it, would never satisfy me, and I had better stay away altogether than be so tantalized.

But now! I could not see it under more fortunate auspices. The Count, by virtue of his high rank and devotion to the Papal See, his intelligence and courtly manners, is a most interesting and invaluable *cicerone*.

And la Contessina! how can I write what I think of her! Indeed, it is time to look into my heart, and ask myself if I am not playing with fire!

I often wish for you, Ed., to see her and share the delight I feel in her society; but, " Friendship is constant in all other things, save in the office and affairs of love." Perhaps it is just as well you are *not* here now for I fear there is no salvation for me—I fear me—Ah, yes! I know it!—I love her!

The words are written, and how strange they look!

I have never breathed them before, but the desire came over me so strongly this evening, when I saw tears in those beautiful eyes, to take her in my arms, and guard her from all sorrow and care, that I can conceal it from myself no longer.

But does she care for me?

Ah, there's the rub! I fear, I fear! Her manner has never been more tender or more cordial than to an intimate friend, and she is so engrossed with the Papal affairs now, that I really believe she can think of nothing else. Therefore, I will not put my future to the test yet, but wait with what patience I may.

CHAPTER III.

OCTOBER 8th.—Rome. At length I tread the sacred soil of the city of the Cæsars!

"Oh, Rome! my country! city of the soul!
The orphans of the heart must turn to thee,
Lone mother of dead empires! and control
In their shut breasts their petty misery.
What are our woes and sufferance? Come and see
The cypress, hear the owl, and plod your way
O'er steps of broken thrones and temples, ye
Whose agonies are evils of a day—
A world is at our feet as fragile as our clay."

So wrote one whose words will be read with rapture through all years to come. But Byron was a Pagan, and saw only as a Pagan.

How completely her own is the title of "Eternal City," for in her meet all the memories of the past. "A mysterious uniting together of two worlds, where the monuments of history, under the double influence of Paganism and Christianity, are collected together." "All roads lead to Rome" is not an empty proverb, for the careful student of ancient and modern history will see how she has influenced in all ages the fate of the nations around her. We see her glory spreading through the years of the early republic and covering, as with an ægis, all the then known world. Then came the emperors, with their luxuries and their crimes, and still the world rolled itself out before them, and their generals came and saw and conquered. In modern times the cross has taken the place of the eagles, the shepherd's crook of the sceptre, but she reigns still—nations bow before her and listen and obey.

I have taken a suite of rooms at the Europa, which look out upon the Piazzi di Spagna with its Fontana della Barcaccia and the magnificent flight of steps leading to the Trinita de Monti, the first church I visited. For, as I shrank away from an introduction to la Contessina, so, after the inevitable first sight of that wonderful dome, I shrank from a nearer view of St. Peter's; nor did I enter it until I had passed and repassed the exterior several times.

The Manzanos, at first, would take no refusal of their offer that I should make their palazzo my home during my stay, but for many reasons, which you, Ed., will understand, I declined. I see them every day, and spend much of my time in their company. But my first visit to St. Peter's interior was alone. I could not bear to have even la Contessina's sweet presence to distract my thoughts on that occasion. Except these two churches, I have seen nothing of Rome in a tourist's sense. My friends have been most anxious, and I cannot but share their anxiety; for what interest have I in the matter, save what will interest her?

The Papal troops were defeated on the 5th, but in an engagement yesterday at Monte Sibieti they recovered all they had lost the day before at Bagnora, whence they were obliged to fall back to Montefiascone.

I have not, as yet, seen the Pope. The Count has had an audience, and a private one is appointed for me to-morrow. I am glad it is to be private, for I shall be better able to form an opinion of the man.

Oct. 10th.—I have seen Pius IX. A fact to be recorded in letters of gold. I must try and give a faithful account of that interview, for I should be sorry to forget its smallest detail.

Count Manzano went with me, and we were ushered into the presence by one of the Papal chamberlains, who dropped the portière as we passed under it and retired. I glanced at the canopied chair, it was vacant, and I was about to speak to the Count, when a movement at one of the deep windows drew my attention, and the Pope was before me! He had been standing in the recess, the depth of which had concealed him.

He wore his usual dress of white flannel, with the cross upon his breast and the ring upon his finger. Tall and dignified in his bearing, with benignity and goodness stamped upon every exquisite feature of his noble face, with the venerable gray hair and the soft, gentle, almost womanly sweet eyes —here was the man whom we would believe the Romans would exchange for a miserable, lecherous apostate such as Victor Emmanuel!

With a bow in return to my deep obeisance and the Count's bent knee, his Holiness stepped forward and seated himself. Count Manzano then presented me. I could but repeat my bow as the Count knelt again and pressed his lips to the cross upon the slipper, for, being a republican, I was not expected to honor his temporal sovereignty by bended knee or kiss upon the hand; being a Protestant, I could have no special reverence for the cross upon his slipper. Therefore I stood.

But the gracious charity of the man prevented any awkwardness in the situation, for, turning to me, he spoke with that wonderful voice of his, thrilling me through and through, asking some kindly question in reference to my visit, and, pleasantly, "What could he do for me?"

Overcome by the mingled emotions which had thronged through my mind during the short time I had stood there, I dropped upon my knee and said:

"Give me your blessing, Holy Father; it is all I ask."

I felt his hand laid on my bowed head, and it seemed to me it was a touch sanctifying my whole being. I bent and kissed the cross upon his slipper, and as I raised my head, I saw there were tears in the old man's eyes. Count Manzano had withdrawn to the window.

The gentle kindness of the Pope's manner I can never forget, nor the silvery sweetness of his remarkable, bell-like voice. Ah! if his enemies could only look upon his gracious presence, they would strive against him no more! The enthusiasm of la Contessina is no wonder to me now; I share it in almost the same degree; and so would you, Ed., were you here—smile as you may when you read this.

Oct. 24th.—This morning a bomb was thrown and exploded in the Piazza Colonna; fortunately there were but few people in the Piazza at the time, and so no lives were lost. But the bomb must have been a signal, or part of a plot, for nearly at the same time the Serristone barracks were blown up and several zouaves killed.

It does seem most outrageous—this secret plotting of a set of lawless desperadoes—and I feel my blood boiling within me. Does Louis Napoleon mean to keep quiet? Poor Spain cannot do much, nor can Austria just now—but France! Certainly the situation of his Holiness is a critical one. The people are devoted to him; so is the army; yet the affair of this morning shows there is treason hidden somewhere, and who can guard against that! In spite of all, the Pope takes a walk as usual through parts of the city every day, unguarded and alone, save for one attendant.

But I do not fear for him; no assassin could look upon the Godlike majesty of the man and do him harm. It is consoling to see the people crowd around him and beg his blessing as he walks in their midst.

But Menotti Garibaldi is at Monte Rotundo, about five miles from Rome. Can the few troops the Pope calls his army defend the city?

A long letter to-day from my father. Knowing how readily I am carried away by my feelings, he begs me to keep out of this Italian broil, and not to interfere or seek to be mixed up with the politics of the country! I must close my journal and answer his letter. I shall assure the old gentleman that, having fought through the war at home, my combative propensities are fully satisfied, and my sword may rest in its scabbard in an inglorious peace for all time to come.

OCTOBER 27th.—Alas! Count Manzano's

predictions and fears were only too well grounded. Garibaldi has escaped from his pretended imprisonment at Caprera and joined his son at Monte Rotundo.

But, as a light in this dark picture, comes the rumor that French troops have sailed from Marseilles and may any moment be expected at Civita Vecchia.

The indignation of la Contessina at the treachery of Victor Emmanuel and her joy at the last news were very great. I dined there to-day, and so lovely did she look in her sorrowful joy, that I could have restrained myself no longer, but would have thrown myself at her feet and besought her to have pity upon me had our tête-a-tête not been interrupted before I reached that length. The Count had left us after dinner, and we had, as usual, been going over duetts, both vocal and instrumental; then she had ceased playing and broken forth into passionate invective against the traitors and the treason. I tried to make her look forward more hopefully than she did, and assured her that now

France had wakened up, all would be well, and in a few moments more the irrevocable words would have been spoken, when the door was thrown open and the servant announced a visitor, in the person of a member of the "*Guard Nobile,*" the Marchese Pellegrini Quarantetti.

La Contessina greeted the young soldier eagerly, and demanded of him the latest intelligence. He, too, spoke hopefully, now that the French troops were coming, and so, after a pleasant evening, we bade her goodnight, leaving her more happy than she had been for a long time.

The Marchese accompanied me to my hotel, where he, too, is staying over night, expecting to return to-morrow to the army. He is a scion of one of the noblest families in Rome, a pupil of the Jesuits, and a young man of great intelligence, cultivation, and most pleasantly genial manners.

And now, old boy, what are you doing with yourself away off in "perfide Albion" —are you writing your journal and thinking of me? Ah! Ed., Ed., what may not happen before the six months are up and we meet at Cologne!

I have told La Contessina all about you, old fellow, and she has made me promise to bring you to Rome before we return to the United States. By-the-bye, she thinks our mutual agreement of not writing a very schoolboyish one. So do I.

Buona notte, e dorme bene! I must write to my father and Eleanore.

To-morrow I have an engagement to dine with la Contessina. I can understand Oswald's feelings now—but had he *such* a Corinne?

CHAPTER IV.

October 28th.

PASSED the morning in making some calls which should have been made earlier, delivering letters, &c., with which one or two of my friends furnished me. It was pleasant to meet Americans, or it would have been had I not been so completely disgusted by their talk upon "the Italian movement," their insane, senseless endorsement of whatever Garibaldi does or says, calling him the "apostle of freedom" and such like titles. Fools! Fools! Will their eyes never be opened!

Equally am I disgusted with the American papers that I receive—editorials and "communications" and letters filled with the most senseless, silly jargon about the "poor priest-ridden Italians and their noble efforts for freedom, under the leadership of that God-inspired man, Garibaldi!" Faugh!

But when such men as William C. Bryant and George W. Curtis lend their pens and minds to the propagation of such trash, and Charles Sumner endorses it, it is simply disgusting. Well, I must be prompt to my engagement with la Contessina, and will give you an account of my drive when I return.

Later.—How strange a thing is destiny!

Had any one told me three months ago, when I was lounging there at home, wishing the hot weather was over, and yet too lazy to leave my comfortable quarters to seek a cooler temperature, that the first of November would find me not only in Rome, but an enlisted soldier of the Pope's and affianced to an Italian of whose existence I was then ignorant, I would have laughed at the idea.

Yet, such is the strange fact, and the drive this afternoon accomplished it.

We had been speaking of the defeat of the Papal forces yesterday at Monte Rotundo, and the dark depths of la Contessina's eyes were troubled and her beautiful lips were drawn with a sad, hopeless expression.

At last she exclaimed:

"Oh, that I were a man and could fight for him!"

In an instant the word was said:

"Contessina—Ginevra! give me but one word and I will be your substitute!"

"You!" She looked at me in unfeigned surprise. Then the thought of what my words implied came to her, and her eyes fell before mine and she sank back into the corner of the carriage.

I waited a little and then said:

"If you will not speak, give me but this little glove, and I will wear it as my gage, like any knight of old. Contessina! tell me at least that I have not offended—that I am not too presumptuous!"

Still she was silent and kept her face turned away, though her bosom heaved. I could say no more, but waited. Presently, finger by finger, she drew off the glove and

THE TWO FRIENDS. 143

laid it on my knee. I took it and pressed it to my lips—her quickly withdrawn hand I did not, could not touch.

Silently we drove on, out through the Porta Pia, and along the beautiful road under the trees of the garden of the Villa Patrizi, towards the church and catacombs of St. Agnes.

After we had gone a little distance, she touched the check and told the coachman to drive to the temporary hospital to which the wounded had been carried.

As we neared it, we saw the Papal carriage and outriders, with the gleaming helmets of the Swiss Guards.

As soon as she found the Pope was at the hospital, the light sprang again into her eyes, and she exclaimed:

"Ah, *bene!* I can now present my soldier!"

"Ginevra!" I said, taking her hand and bending over her to look into her face, "Have you no word for me. Am I worth no thought in your mind, save as one soldier more for the Pope?"

Again her eyes drooped and she withdrew her hand, speaking very low:

"What can I say, Signor Gwynne, save that I thank you?"

"Is that all! No—call me by my name once—let me hear it from your lips to rock the sounds in my heart forever. Say Luigi!"

But she would not. I could not understand her strange mood, and before anything more could be said the carriage stopped.

I helped her to alight and led her into the building. The door of a room near the entrance was partly open and we entered. Here we found his Holiness bending over the body of a zouave who had just breathed his last: the man had been brought in insensible, and had only recovered sufficiently to receive the last offices of the Church.

There was a hush of silence in the room, unbroken save by the silvery tones of the Pope as he recited the "*De profundis clamavi ad te, Domine.*"

We all knelt while he repeated the prayers for the dead. I had never heard the beautiful service before, and in my then excited state it made a very strong impression upon me.

As he rose from his knees, the Pope, with his own hand, drew the cloth over the face of the dead man and turned sadly away.

La Contessina beckoned me into an adjoining room, and thither his Holiness came. He greeted us with a smile, but there was a sad and anxious expression on his noble face.

"*Ah, figlia mia!*" he exclaimed, "our burden grows heavier every day! There is an engagement to-day at Terracina—pray God the victory may be ours! But my poor people! My poor children! When will this bloodshed cease?"

"God only knows the end, Holy Father! But I bring you a recruit, one who takes the place I cannot in your ranks. Will your Holiness receive him?"

"*Il Signor Americano!* Ah, my son, you are of neither our country nor our faith. Have you reflected upon what you do?"

"I have done nothing hastily, Holy

Father. My heart and hopes are in the matter. Having served both in the ranks and as an officer in our own civil war, I am ready to use the experience so gained as your Holiness may see fit to direct it. I place myself here at your disposal."

As I spoke I sank upon my knee and pressed the beautiful hand he held out to me to my lips.

"Well, be it so, my son, and God bless you!"

When we were again alone, la Contessina resumed her silent aspect, and I dared make no attempt to disturb it. It was an uncomfortable drive back to the city, and I felt still more straugely when, having seen la Contessina to her father's door, I found myself once more in my own quarters.

We parted more like strangers than what I suppose we are, affianced lov—no—I cannot say lovers—and yet she did not reject; strange—strange!

Am I the same man who left these rooms a few short hours ago? I can hardly believe that I have not lain upon the sofa and dreamed it all! And yet I know it is true —and to-morrow a new life, a strange existence begins for me.

I cannot sleep. I ought by rights to seek the Count and tell him of my new resolve and of what I dared to tell his daughter. But I must write to poor Eleanore and to my father.

Ah! there the task is not an easy one. My father will not hear my news patiently!

OCT. 29th.—The Papal troops surrounded Nicotera and took some prisoners yesterday near Terracina. The French have landed at Civita Vecchia, but Garibaldi is at Basina del Colombo, only three miles from the city gate.

This morning I received from the Pope a beautiful sword and my commission as Lieutenant and aide to General Polkè. This pomp and panoply of war and the resuming a rôle I thought I had laid aside forever, takes me back to the dark days so lately passed at home.

I sought la Contessina this morning, but she was excused on the plea of indisposition. Her father I saw, however, and he congratulated me upon my account of what passed yesterday kindly. So I have nothing to fear in that quarter. Have been busy with my new duties all day. The French are expected here to-morrow.

Night.—Not a glimpse of la Contessina have I had to-day to soothe my low spirits: for I have been dull and sad, albeit so busy.

Oct. 30th.—The French entered Rome to-day. How glad the populace were to see them and how they shouted vivas! We met and escorted them through the city, and here I am in a tent near Tivoli, once more a soldier. But Ginevra's—la Contessina's behaviour is very strange. I have not seen her since that eventful night. Ah, well!

CHAPTER V.

WE attack the Garibaldians to-morrow. I was in the city on business this morning and sought the Palazzo Manzano. The Count was at home and sent for la Contessina, else I doubt that I would have seen her.

He kindly left me before she obeyed his summons, and I had a last look upon her face, a last touch of her hand, a last word from her lips, alone.

When she entered the room it was with a slightly flushed cheek, and I judged that her father had awaited her in the hall and told her whom she would meet—perhaps insisted upon her granting me the interview. She was reserved in her manner, but made many enquiries about my camp life and the chances of success to-morrow.

When I rose to take leave, I think I surprised her not a little when I begged her pardon for any pain I had caused her and for my presumption. I asked her to forget that drive completely, as I would never presume again: telling her I had not regretted or changed the decision made then—my fealty was given to the Holy Father and I would not withdraw it. One last favor I begged, however—that I might be allowed to keep the glove she had given me, not as a troth-pledge, but as a treasure, in my eyes beyond all price. Then I asked her to remember me in her prayers sometimes and to think kindly of me if I fell.

As I spoke the dark eyes were troubled, and as they rested on me there was a softness —a new expression I had not noticed before. She did not interrupt me. When I took her hand and asked her again if she would pray for me, her only answer was a motion of the stately head. I bent over the hand I held and pressed it to my lips, then left her without another look or word.

I feel strangely to-night—not as I ever felt before on the eve of a battle. Is it ominous? Ah, Ed., how different were some of our vigils in the swamps of the Chickahominy and the wilds of East Tennessee! I have written to Eleanore and to my father what may be my last words.

It is late, but

> "I cannot sleep, my fervid brain
> Calls up the vanished past again,
> And throws its misty splendors deep
> Into the pallid realms of sleep!
> A breath from that far distant shore
> Comes freshening ever more and more,
> And wafts o'er intervening seas
> Sweet odors from the Hesperides!"

The camp is perfectly quiet except a light in the chaplain's tent, where the good priest is busy hearing confessions. What consolation these Catholics find in every observance of their religion, and how it does indeed, as la Contessina said, meet every emergency of life!

Nov. 4th—Two o'clock in the morning. How will my father receive the news I have now to tell him? What will Ed. Mainwaring, with all his New England Puritanism thick upon him, say, if we meet in Cologne in March next? As I write the words, I can scarcely believe three or four hours have sufficed to change so thoroughly my whole life! *I am a Roman Catholic!*

The act will never be repented, for " what doth it profit a man to gain the whole world and lose his own soul?"

But I must leave a record of the events of this night for those who may be interested to know how my last moments were spent should I fall to-morrow.

Restless and ill at ease after writing to my father and Eleanore and posting my journal as I thought for the last time, I wandered aimlessly out into the camp, beneath the canopy of the peaceful heaven.

The lights were all out save in the tent of the chaplain, and the glimmer of his lamp drew me strongly. I walked towards it, and just as I approached a soldier came out and turned with a quick step away. As I drew nearer the Padre Alesandro himself raised the door covering and stood for an instant looking upward. His lips moved in prayer, and the peculiar light from the Italian sky, which is neither starlight nor moonlight, irradiated his fine face. I hesitated to disturb him, but in another instant he saw and greeted me.

We spoke together some time upon the chances of to-morrow's fight, and gradually, drawn out by the holy man's kindly sympathy, I gave words in part to the mood that was upon me.

To my expressions of despondency he opposed the hopefulness that should animate a truly Christian soul; to my doubts of any future good he spoke of the ardent faith which had supported the martyrs in their sufferings, and which animated the hearts of the men around us, who were ready to give their lives in testimony against the false spirit of the age, as truly martyrs as those who were torn to pieces by wild beasts in the amphitheatre or died beneath the tortures of the imperial tyrants; to my question, like Pilate's, "What is truth?" he pointed to the Rock upon which Christ built His Church and the promise that "the gates of hell should not prevail against it" which He, "the Way, the Truth, and the Life," had given. I had heard many of his arguments, or similar ones, from the lips of la Contessina, as well as in several calm, dispassionate conversations with the Count, and had acknowledged the truth of them, and begun to think that if *there were a necessity for*, or if *there were* a revealed religion, the Roman Catholic Church made the most logical claims to it. Therefore, it was not strange that, overcome by the words of the holy man, my own yearnings in that hour of darkness for some glimpse of the light, and the conviction that it was only to be found in the Catholic Church which was forced upon me, I bowed my head and exclaimed, "I believe, Lord help Thou my unbelief."

Having no certainty that the rite of baptism had ever been conferred upon me, neither of my parents being members of any Church, Padre Alesandro imparted to me the sacrament.

Truly do I understand and taste "the peace which passeth all understanding," and I look forward to what the morrow may bring as the perfecting of my consecration.

And, oh, Ginevra! loved now with a fonder, because a nearer love—but I must not think of her!

Now, having sealed this and directed it to la Contessina in case I fall to-morrow—that she may know I loved her to the end, but died for a higher, holier feeling than love of any mortal; that my life was given gladly, freely, for the cause I had embraced so late, trusting that I might be received, even though I came at the eleventh hour; hoping, while my fall throws no permanently sad cloud upon her life, she will give my memory some tender thoughts, my soul some kindly prayers to help it through the Dark Valley—I will try to sleep, perhaps for the last time.

CHAPTER VI.

JANUARY 2d, 1868, Thursday.

IT was not my last sleep, but it came very near it. My experience of the Papal service was short and not very sweet.

Before the battle had well begun, I carried an order to the artillery officer, and dismounted to assist in sighting one of the guns, when my horse was struck by a shot full in the chest, and, rearing, fell over upon me.

I remember the fearfully human cry the poor animal gave, felt his body pressing down upon me, an excruciating pain in my breast, a rush of something into my throat, a choking sensation, and nothing more—for many days.

When I awoke from the sleep that broke my fever, I was conscious of resting upon a delightfully comfortable bed and the pressure of a soft hand upon my brow. Then a pair of soft lips dropped a kiss upon my forehead, there was a rustle of woman's garments, and a door closed gently. I needed no light in the darkened room, no mentioned name to tell me who it was, and my heart rose with a triumphant thankfulness to Him who had spared and blessed me. I saw the room I was in was not the one I had occupied at the "Europa," and I guessed at once that I was an inmate of the Palazzo Manzano.

I must have been partially conscious during my illness, for I was not at all surprised when Eleanore entered the room softly and stood by my bedside. But I noticed she was in black, and while I wondered, I was too weak to ask the reason, partly supposing it to be the dress or uniform of her "*pension.*"

She slipped her hand into mine and bent and kissed me, then said quietly:

"You must not talk, Louis; the doctor says your life depends on the greatest care."

I pressed her hand, closed my eyes and turned my head away. The baptism of that remembered kiss made my life very precious, and I would get well if God so willed.

The days dragged on wearily. Eleanore seldom left me, and quietly told me of the victory we had gained at Mentana, and of the peace which had been undisturbed since then; of Menotti Garibaldi's wound and capture, and of his father's imprisonment at Spezzia; but she gave me no explanation of the black dress she wore, nor did she mention having heard from our father. At both I wondered, but I was too weak to connect the two or to ask any questions.

Count Manzano came to my room every day, and the Padre Alesandro often. During all these visits I could not speak save with my eyes, for strict silence was enjoined, and I was forbidden to use my arms much or make the exertion of writing.

Several times I had recognized, upon awakening from my daily sleep, the *presence* which had greeted first my recovered faculties, but the soft, light kiss was given ere I was fully aroused; and when I was so, either I was alone or Eleanore appeared at the least movement.

Weeks I lay thus, gradually gaining strength, and at length I was able to sit up, and could once more use my powers of speech slightly. During these weeks I noticed that Eleanore and the Count were careful not to recur to anything in which I had taken part, in their conversations. They kept me *au courant* with matters of local and present interest; of the irruption of Mount Vesuvius, which during the second week of December afforded a spectacle of unusual grandeur; of the arrival of the remains of poor Maximilian, and of the organization of a cabinet at Florence by General Manabrea, with Reale as Minister of War. At last Eleanore told me of the search for me after the battle, of la Contessina's intense anxiety, and how she had joined in the search herself; that it was she who had found me under my horse and the debris of a gun carriage. The instant after my fall, a bomb having exploded upon the very cannon I had sought to point, killing the gunners and knocking the carriage all to pieces, it seemed a special interposition of Providence that the gun itself had not fallen upon me, completing the work my noble horse had so sadly begun. They had carried me by easy stages back to the city, to the Palazzo Manzano, and sent instantly for Eleanore, la Contessina herself writing to my father.

Still la Contessina gave me no sign or token that she knew of, or cared for, my presence in the house—only—ah, there I needed no interpreter—those mysterious kisses were bestowed upon me on awakening from every sleep; and once I awoke sooner than usual, and found her at my bedside. I closed my eyes again, fearful that she had noticed that I was not asleep, but she had not, and when the usual time came for me to awake, and I opened my eyes again, she was gone.

Then came, as soon as I was strong enough to bear it, the intelligence of my father's death.

He began to make arrangements to sail for Europe on the receipt of my first letter; that of la Contessina only quickened his movements. He reached Marseilles in three weeks after the battle, and was there stricken down with fever, the result of fatigue and over-excitement. Finding himself unable to proceed, he telegraphed the United States consul at Rome, and Eleanore went to him, Count Manzano accompanying her. A few days after her arrival my father died.

And so they buried him under the soil of sunny France, on the shores of the "tideless sea," and then returned to watch my fevered wanderings. Poor little Eleanore!

But I cannot induce Eleanore to tell me what his feelings towards me were. Had he left a last loving message for me she would surely have given it. When I ask her she evades the question, and will give me no satisfaction. Ah, well! If he died angry with me, I know his intention was pure; he sincerely thought I was wrong, and he knows now that I was right!

This is what the last two months have brought me: The father I left, not young, it is true, but promising many years yet of life not six months ago, now sleeps his last sleep beneath an alien sky; and I, who before that was free from every physical ill, have tossed for six weeks on what threatened to be a bed of death, to arise from it with a shattered constitution, and a weakened frame which can bear not the least strain upon it.

But have I received no compensation for my lost strength? Ah, yes, the greatest. The gift of the *true faith*, and the love of Ginevra Manzano. For she does love me, silent as she still is.

JAN. 15.—I wrote too long the last time they let me have a pen; to-day I have promised to be more careful. Ah, these poor lungs that bleed at every exertion!

Yesterday Eleanore was twenty-one; it was a sad birthday, spent at my bedside. This morning she was absent a long time, and returned with an air about her of great satisfaction. While she was gone the Count sat with me, and kept me amused for a long while with anecdote and reading of the papers. Seemingly by chance he introduced his daughter's name, but I know it was to give me the opportunity of speaking of her. I did not let it slip, by any means.

I told him how I had released her from her engagement to me in the last interview I had had with her, but that I had not ceased to love her; indeed, loved her far more devotedly and entirely. He did not know of this, and told me it accounted for much that was strange in Ginevra's behavior. He had wondered at her anxiety about my fate and subsequent recovery, which she could not conceal, while he had never been able to induce her to enter my room when there was a chance of my being awake, and she had, as I grew better, tried to ignore her previous distress, and seldom mentioned my name.

What happiness it was for me to know this—she does love me—and it is only the barrier I myself have raised which keeps her from me—before I sleep to-night that barrier will be no more.

By degrees I found out the reason of Eleanore's absence this morning. My father, upon receiving my letter announcing my having taken service in the Papal army, was so angry that he made a new will before leaving home, excluding me entirely. Eleanore begged him earnestly, during the few days he survived her arrival at Marseilles, to alter or destroy it, and told him she would do so herself. But he had taken steps to prevent any such action on her part by leaving a copy with his lawyer at home.

This was why she always avoided the subject.

This morning she went to the United States consul, laid the matter before him, and by his advice executed a deed making over to me my full share.

My dear, loving Eleanore!

And my dear, dear father! May the God who sees all hearts, and reads their inmost thoughts, pardon and reward him! I am able to sit up almost all day now and enjoy the view from my windows very much, and certainly none could be of more varied interest or of greater beauty.

The palazzo is situated on the declivity of the Esquiline, where the gardens of Heliogabalus are said to have been. To the east, as I look from my windows, Monte Cavi, where Romulus, amid the assembled tribes, inaugurated the religion of Latium, raises its head. To the left of this lies the ancient Tusculum, with its suggestions of Cicero, and its ruins; then Tivoli and its Casealette, among the Sabine hills, and the memories of the sufferings endured there only a few months ago. The Mons Sacer, the asylum of the populace when flying from the tyranny of the politicians, is the next object. The mountain of Soracte

"from out the plain
Heaves like a long-swept wave about to break,
And on the curl hangs pending,"

and the Campagna, in the neighborhood of Civita Vecchia, closes the picture as far as the eye can reach on that side. The Mediterranean mingles its blue waters with the scarce bluer sky. Then comes Ostia, and then the ridge of mountains again, with Monte Cavi towering above them, and at last, in the heights, the castle of Gandolfa, the country home of the Popes. Within this circle, which bounds the horizon, there are scattered through the Campagna some of the few monuments of antiquity which survive to this day. To the right is the tomb of Cecilia Metella; next the Aqueduct of Claudius; to the left the wondrous ruins of the villa of Adrian and the tomb of Plautius Lucanus. In the centre of this vast plain the Eternal City lies before me, surrounded by walls said to have been built by Aurelian, but which are nearly all restorations.

Feb 1.—I little thought ever to make another entry in this book.

The day after, the 16th, I was sitting,

propped up by pillows, by the open window, breathing the balmy air of the Roman spring, for so I might call it, the sun was so warm, and drinking in the never-wearying beauty of the scene, with the sun shining on the domes and spires of the city. My mind was full of conflicting thoughts, and was I going over the events of the past months, and wondering what Ginevra's feelings were when she read my letter, when I heard a movement at my side, and a voice:

"Caro mio! Luigi carissimo!"

She was standing near me, lovelier than ever, with the glad yet subdued light of love in her beautiful eyes.

I sprang up and held out my arms.

She came to me. I felt her soft arms round my neck—a kiss, and then that strange rush in my throat and strangulation, and as I fell I saw the terrified expression in her face. I knew no more.

I found afterwards that the hemorrhage had returned, and I had deluged her with my blood. After this I was very ill for some days, and my life was despaired of.

And now the doctor says this chill, damp weather which has come upon Rome is the worst thing for me, and I must go to Sicily. He will not promise me three months more of life if I do not.

I could not go alone, nor were my friends willing that I should, with only little Eleanore as nurse and companion. She, too, shrank from the responsibility, and begged Ginevra to accompany us. The Count cannot leave Rome just now; la Contessina could not go without him, unless—in short, we are to be married to-morrow, and start the next day. It will be a strange ceremony, for I cannot yet stand up. We will be married very quietly, with no pomp or display; my condition, as well as my father's recent death, will prevent anything of the kind.

The rector of the American College will perform the ceremony.

So I must not write any more to-night, for fear of consequences. Nor can I put in words the peace and happiness that fill my heart.

CHAPTER VII.

GIRGENTI, SICILY, February 14.

ONCE more I open my little book. My wife—how strange the word looks!—my wife having read what I have written, wishes me to continue the journal, not that it will ever greet the eyes of Mainwaring (I have great fun in trying to get Ginevra's sweet lips round that Hubbish name)—parts of it are too sacred for any but our own—but for our own satisfaction in after years, when we are gray and wrinkled, and all that is passing now so vividly real shall seem like a dream.

We have a lovely villa on the heights above the town, commanding a beautiful view over the dark blue water, with the vessels of all shapes and sizes floating over its surface. Certainly I am blessed, and have no desire for any change. The hemorrhage has not returned, and I feel perceptibly improved just in our short stay.

The journey from Rome here was very interesting. The Count was fortunate enough to secure for me a yacht, which a young Englishman had been obliged to leave at Civita Vecchia, having been recalled by some family trouble. "It is an ill wind which blows nobody any good," and while I sincerely hope his difficulties will be settled comfortably, I am very much obliged to him for the beautiful little craft he was reluctantly enough, I can imagine, forced to leave behind him.

My physician ordered me to the southern part of the island, so we did not go to Palermo, but sailed first for Naples, lying at anchor for a few hours in that most perfect bay, where

> " Ischia smiles
> O'er liquid miles
> And yonder bluest of the isles,
> Calm Capri waits,
> Her sapphires gates
> Beguiling to her bright estates; "

past the Lipari islands, Stromboli's "lone volcanic isle," with its infernal legends.

Then we entered the mouth of the Taro, and Scylla's storied rocks rose abruptly on our left, projecting into the sea, a spur of the rugged mountains of Calabria, which rise from the margin of the strait to an almost Alpine elevation.

On the other side was Cape Peloris, where Hannibal put his pilot to death, suspecting him of treachery in taking him through the Taro, finding out his error too late. The channel is at this point about six thousand yards across, but grows gradually wider towards Messina. As we neared that city we saw the famous Charybdis, a whirlpool formed by the meeting of the two currents of the strait, and the harbor. Its depth is from seventy to ninety fathoms, and presents a pool of eddies strong enough to whirl around a seventy-four-gun ship, and of course was destruction unfailing to the small undecked vessels of the ancients. And so we coasted along, past Messina, and then under the shadow of Mount Etna, for miles. We passed up the southern coast until the charming situation of Girgenti decided us to raise our tent there for the present. This was the ancient Agrigentum, and stands on an immense platform everywhere defended by precipitous rocks, the highest part 1,200 feet above the sea.

Here we cast anchor, and while I sent Gianbattisto to engage rooms for us at the inn, Ginevra and I sat on the deck and drank in the beauty of the scene. It was morning, and the sun shining brightly, the air so balmy and fresh compared with the damp chilliness of Rome. After a little delay, Gianbattisto returned and informed us that the inn being full he had sought and found apartments with a private family, beneath whose friendly roof we were sheltered and made at home before nightfall.

The next few days were spent in "house hunting," we would call it at home, by Eleanore and Ginevra, under the care and guidance of Gianbattisto. They enjoyed the excursions immensely, and gave me most graphic accounts of the palazzos and palazzettas they had been introduced to on their return every afternoon.

At length they decided upon one, between the old city and the new, commanding a splendid view, and into it we moved, with something the feeling of children going into a new play-house, notwithstanding the regrets of our kind hosts that we would leave them before our house was in perfect order, and now awaited the coming of our household goods from Rome.

The yacht still rides at anchor below us, and, as soon as I am well enough, we propose many a day's pleasure by means of it.

FEB. 15th.—I have made Ginevra explain at length her strange behavior before the affair of Mentana.

The cause was simple enough: she did not love me.

Just as I supposed.

She had a sincere friendship for me, and enjoyed my society exceedingly (!) but no warmer feeling had arisen in her breast when I took her so completely by surprise during our drive.

At first, she was about to decline the honor I had done her, but suddenly the thought came to her, that if she could not serve the Pope in one way, she could in another: she could not join his army herself, but if by the sacrifice of her freedom she could gain a soldier for him, she had no right to lose the opportunity.

She was disappointed, too, that my enthusiasm did not lead me to wish to serve his Holiness for himself alone, or from a full conviction of the justice of his cause, and no other.

It was not until I released her, or informed her that I held her no longer bound —that I would give my life for Pius IX without any hope of reward from her love, that she began to care for me.

When they brought her my journal, which, being addressed to her, she opened, and when she read my love on every page, so unquestionably shown, and above all when they brought her word that I was killed, she needed nothing further to show her the true state of her heart, she knew *then* that she loved, and *could not* lose me.

Our plan of meeting at Cologne must be given up.

I could not stand the change of air, or the railroad journey. At first I was in hopes to get to Marseilles to meet Ed., but the old fellow will have to come to me here.

Feb. 22d.—Shall I ever celebrate another Washington's birthday in the United States? I think not. After seeing Ed., and as soon as I am able, we will return to my native land for a short time to take Eleanore home and settle my affairs there.

The spirit of the age—the "progressive ideas" of the present time, as it is the affectation to call them, are too rampant in the United States. The "idea" seems to be to get rid of all that can excite the nobler feelings of the soul, and reduce everything to a harsh materialism, which laughs to scorn any acknowledgement of a higher power than human will and understanding, and does not suit me. I never was a great favorite in "society," and my change of religion will, of course, build a wall of adamant between my friends and me; the climate will not suit my poor, damaged lungs, and, altogether, I think Italy is to be my future abiding place.

Eleanore has many relations and old friends to see, and she can take her choice, or indulge in the luxury of two homes, one there, the other here. But I do not think the New World will keep her long; if I guess rightly, the Contessa Novera will bid adieu to America next winter, and make, with her husband and her brother, her home beneath Italian skies.

The more I see of this lovely country the more I love it, and after residing any time in Rome, any other place seems "flat, stale, and unprofitable."

"Age cannot wither her, nor custom stale
  Her infinite variety."

Besides, the very air breathed by Pius IX is hallowed! How I thank God that the grand old man has triumphed! His enemies in their pride are stricken to the earth, and cower before him.

My enthusiastic Ginevra's words seem true: "Rome is the Pope's, and the Pope is Rome's." It seems impossible to separate them.

MARCH 1st.—This morning I made my First Communion. The gift of faith came to me in a strange way, but I, none the less, thank God for it! And I pray the boon may never be withdrawn. Health seems returning to me slowly but, I hope, surely. If one could get well anywhere, it would be here.

MARCH 5th.—Have written to Mainwaring to join me here. I did not tell him anything beyond the mere fact, that "circumstances over which I have had no control" would prevent my fulfilling my part of the contract to meet at Cologne, and begged him to come to Sicily.

I am nervous about the meeting. Not that I regret, or would have one circumstance—(yes, *one*—if I could but hear my father's voice in love and foregiveness! But I try not to think of that—) altered. Still, the last six months have held so much of my life, there has come such a change over my inner man, that I am not surprised to find there is so little in the outer, and I cannot help but be anxious as to this meeting.

It is strange, after an ordinary quiet life of years, with nothing happening from one day to another out of the regular routine of events, to have, in a few weeks or months, the steady sequence completely broken up, and circumstances, each one enough for a lifetime, crowding upon one with the rush and rapidity of an avalanche! These last six months seem years to me, and I feel as if I were entirely another being.

As Ed. takes my change in religion, or

rather, my awakening to the necessity of *any*, and my embracing Catholicity, I shall judge how it will be received at home.

MARCH 8th.—Six months ago to-day we parted in London, and Ed. will be here to-morrow. To-day, I received a medal from the Pope, and a brevet of nobility—shall I call it so? Henceforth, I write "*Cavaliere*" before my name.

These two excitements this morning brought on the hemorrhage again, only slightly, however, and I have promised Ginevra to keep very quiet. She becomes very much terrified at the thought of my never getting better, and if she could prevent it I would never make the least exertion. She has importuned me often to give up my journal, and at last I have promised to do so, as she thinks the bending over the desk to write injures me, and she has promised to keep one herself if it will be any satisfaction to me.

I often think of the sketch I made of

what my wife should be, upon that eventful night last August, which was the turning point of my destiny, and compare the ideal with the reality.

Is she not all I pictured?

Aye, and more! Daily do I thank God for the treasure of her love; each day reveals some new charm, some stronger claim upon my deep and fond devotion. A little poem of Owen Meredith's, which I read to her to-day, says all I can but poorly express:

> "The love that deep within me lies
>   Unmoved, abides in conscious power;
> Yet in the heaven of thy sweet eyes
>   It varies every hour.
>
> A look from thee will flush the cheek:
>   A word of thine awaken tears;
> And, ah, in all I do and speak,
>   How frail my love appears.
>
> In yonder tree, belov'd, whose boughs
>   Are households both to earth and heaven,
> Whose leaves have murmur'd of our vows
>   To many a balmy even.
>
> The branch that wears the liveliest green,
>   Is shaken by the restless bird;
> The leaves that nighest heaven are seen,
>   By every breeze are stirred.

THE TWO FRIENDS.

> But storms may rise and thunders roll,
>   Nor move the giant roots below;
> So, from the bases of the soul,
>   My love for thee doth grow.
>
> It seeks the heaven and trembles there,
>   To every light and passing breath;
> But from the heart no storm can tear
>   Its rooted growth beneath."

To-morrow, to-morrow! Once more I shall clasp the hand of my friend, once more hear his voice; will it be for the last time? Ah! Ed., Ed., have you the faintest idea of the feelings with which I look forward to our meeting?

But of course you have not; how could you?

PART FOURTH.

SICILY.

CHAPTER I.

AGAIN it is an evening which might be called a summer one, so mild and balmly is the air, although it is March, not August. But the spot upon which I again introduce the two friends is Sicily, not the banks of the Ohio.

Once more Mainwaring and Gwynne are together, and alone; and as they stand, with their arms thrown over each other's shoulders, gazing out upon the lovely landscape spread before them from the balcony of Gwynne's villa on the site of one of the temples of ancient Agrigentum, let us see what the last six months has brought of change, physically.

Of equal height, and that rather above than under the altitude of their fellow-men, both are thinner than they were last summer; but Mainwaring's form shows the greater falling off. Were it light enough to see, there would be found many a silver thread in his brown locks. The beauty which played hide and seek over his irregular features, making it so difficult to place its source, is changed, but, if anything, increased. The "shadowed" eyes are dark and beautiful as ever, but there is an expression in them which tells of much suffering undergone, a hard battle fought and won. The face is thinner and paler even than it was before, but the intellectual beauty is all there.

Gwynne looks like a man who has had a hard tussle for life and conquered. His perfect beauty of feature and expression is etherialized, while not one iota of it is lost. He, too, is pale; but there is evidence of a renewed life springing up within him, and he will soon be able to throw off all the trammels of invalidism.

Mainwaring had arrived about half an

hour ago, Louis had met him alone on the balcony, and they had not yet entered the house. Nor had they spoken many words. Hand clasped hand, and eye looked into eye for welcome, and then they had thrown their arms around each other's shoulders, as in their boyish days, and walked to the balcony's end in silence. Presently, upon the soft evening air rose the exquisite melody of a woman's richly-cultivated voice:

> "Ellege de natura
> Che a compatir ci muove
> Che prova una scentura
> Che voi provammo ancor.
> O sia chi amore in noi
> La formiglianza accenda,
> Oh sia, che più s'intenda
> Nel suo l'altrui dolor."

It was one of Mestastasia's sweetest songs, and a great favorite with Ginevra. At the sound of her voice Gwynne had started and glanced at Mainwaring. The latter was listening in unfeigned enjoyment.

"What a beautiful voice!" he exclaimed, when she had finished.

"Yes, and she is a beautiful woman!" replied Gwynne.

"Who is the singer, amico? An inmate—a fellow-boarder?" asked Mainwaring.

"We have much to tell each other, old boy!" replied Louis. "Yes, the singer is an inmate—a fellow-boarder—but she is also—my wife!"

"Your wife! Louis, you are joking!"

"Not by any means, Ed.; and now it is time to seek her and report ourselves."

He turned as he spoke and led the way through one of the open windows into a saloon furnished with all the elegance which wealth, assisted by refined taste, could command. Across this room and a wide hall Mainwaring followed into a sort of arcade—an apartment opened on two sides to the air by wide arches instead of windows. This was their favorite sitting-room, and here Ginevra and Eleanore were waiting for them.

"Here's our old friend, Eleanore!" exclaimed Gwynne, as he entered, "and Mainwaring, this is my wife, Ginevra."

The meeting could not be otherwise than

awkward, although Ginevra's ready tact did away with the feeling as quickly as possible. She watched her husband anxiously, knowing how he had dreaded this time, and fearing it would have a bad effect upon him; but though Louis was nervous—how nervous he and she only knew—he kept up better than she expected, and tried in every way to conceal and overcome the feeling. They had not time to do more than exchange a few commonplaces when the servant announced that the evening meal was ready, by throwing open the *portière* which hung in an archway on one of the two sides of the room which did not open upon the outer air, and revealing, in a similar apartment, the table set with Southern delicacies in gleaming glass and silver. They gathered around the board, and then, ere they took their seats, there was a pause; Ginevra made the sign of the cross without any hesitation; Eleanore stood with bowed head, "saying grace" in her own way; Louis made a movement to raise his hand to his forehead, then hesitated, and glanced at his friend; Edgar had been about to do the same, when he saw the motion made by Gwynne, and paused in amazement. The two looked at each other bewildered, and then Louis said:

"I did not propose, Ed., to begin a history of the last six months until after awhile, but a part of it is forced upon me now: I am a Catholic."

He turned pale as he spoke, and Ginevra hurried around to his side.

"It is nothing, dear," he said. "You know how I have dreaded this announcement; it is just as well to have it over."

And as he spoke he glanced anxiously at Mainwaring.

He, too, was pale, and his long, slender fingers were clenched around the back of the chair upon which he rested.

"Is it so, Louis? Is it, indeed, so? Oh, amico, you cannot know what a weight you have lifted from my heart! I, too, have dreaded this meeting, for I, too, am a Catholic!"

"You! Edgar! But—." He sank into a chair and pressed his handkerchief to his lips; when he withdrew it, there were blood-stains on it.

"Luigi, caro!" exclaimed Ginevra, "you have hurt yourself. Oh, pray, pray, for my sake, keep quiet."

"It is nothing, dearest," replied her husband. "I will be all right in a few moments; but I must go to my room."

He left the apartment, followed by Ginevra, and then Eleanore spoke:

"Louis has been dreading this meeting extremely, Edgar; he so feared the change in his religious sentiments would break up and destroy your friendship for him."

"Just as I felt. But when, how, and where did this marvelous change take place, Nora?"

"Ah! that I must not tell. He wishes to give you the history of the past six months himself."

"But you—your father—how?"

"My father is dead, Edgar," she replied simply.

"Dead! Oh, forgive me, Nora!"

She was silent a few moments, and then said:

"Yes, he died quite suddenly last November; but Louis will tell you all. If the change in Louis' religious feelings astonishes you, how much more must not the change in you astonish us, for you were always more bitter in your dislike to the professions of, and prejudiced in your feelings towards, Catholics than he."

"Yes, I know; and for that very reason I imagine my struggles have been greater than his. I can guess pretty nearly," he added, laughing, "the moving power in his conversion."

"Ginevra? Yes, you are right. And isn't she lovely?"

"Indeed she is, and I can understand, knowing Louis as well as I do, that love for her would overcome all obstacles. But how do you like the change?"

"It has not altered Louis' feelings towards me, and as long as that is the case, and he is happy, it makes no difference."

At this moment Ginevra returned to say Louis would be with them in a few moments, and that they were not to wait for him.

That evening it was late before the friends parted, and when they did, their stories were told, and the ties of friendship and affection, which had bound them so long together, strengthened for all time.

CHAPTER II.

EVEN in Sicily March is sometimes a blustering month, and the next day was bleak and stormy; a keen March wind swept along the rocks by the sea and moaned itself away in the hills and rocky cliffs back of the villa; yet, withal, there was a beauty all its own over the island.

As the family sat together in the saloon overlooking the shore, they could see on one side heavy green waves beating on the beach, while the sea stretched away until lost in the lowering clouds on the other. The straggling modern town of Girgenti, which lay upon the ledge of rock below them and formed, with its small, modern-built houses, a strange contrast to the columns and half-ruined temples of Agrigentum all around them; and beyond, the road leading up into the open country, bounded by a hedge of prickly cactus. Quite near them, almost, in fact, adjoining the house, were some remnants of an ancient temple. Mainwaring drew Gwynne's attention to them and asked what they were.

"That is the ruin of the temple of Æsculapius, Ed. History makes frequent mention of this, you remember, in the accounts of Agrigentum, particularly in relation to the siege it suffered from the Romans during the first Punic war. Polybius tells us of the statue of Apollo—a masterpiece of the Greek sculptor Myron—which this temple possessed, and which was carried away at the time the Carthagenians ravaged Agrigentum.

"Yes, I remember. Scipio recovered the statue when he became master of Carthage, and restored it to the Agrigentines; but Verres again profaned the temple and thus inspired one of the most brilliant passages with which the eloquence of Cicero overwhelmed the tyrant and despoiler of Sicily."

"Your historical lore is correct, as usual,

mon sage, but perhaps you don't know that the "marble halls" in which you are now domiciled are built partly with the broken remnants of the temple," replied Gwynne. "In a room on the other side of the house, which we keep closed, having no use for it, I can show you two columns, now built into the wall of the house, which formerly belonged to the pronaos of the temple."

"I dare say the whole island is full of interesting objects. Have you been to see Etna yet?"

"No. I was too ill when we first came over to go anywhere; now we can go together, a *partie carrée.*"

A few days after Mainwaring's arrival at Girgenti, a letter from Maitland reached him, having been forwarded from Cologne:

MAITLAND RECTORY, March 1, 1868.

MY DEAR MAINWARING:

"*Chacun à son gout,*" mon ami, and I suppose yours must be indulged. I confess I read your letter with feelings of great disgust and disappointment, but if you are happy, no one has a right to interfere, least of all I.

If you come to Scotland again I shall be happy to see you at the Rectory, if you will care to trust yourself among heretics and unbelievers.

My regards to Gwynne and best wishes for your enjoyment of your Continental tour.

Yours,
A. M. MAITLAND.

When Mainwaring read this, he felt that he had received his conge from the Maitlands, and regretted both the feeling which could prompt it and the result. His regret, however, was not as poignant as it might have been had he found things as he feared he would with Louis; and the weeks he spent on the island were happy ones in every way; he was happier far than he had ever been before.

They explored the island, and climbed even to the crater of Etna. They luxuriated in rare and beautiful floral treasures, with which, as the weather grew warmer, the earth began to teem. Gwynne grew daily stronger under the united influence of the balmy air and the perfect happiness which had returned to him. But Mainwaring remained very much in the same state physically as when he reached the island, and although he did not complain, they were all anxious about him.

Padre Moroni, the priest whose church in Girgenti the Gwynnes had attended since their arrival in the island, was a welcome and frequent visitor. He was a marked contrast to Mr. Baine; still Mainwaring began to be as eager for his coming as he had been, in London, for the hours appointed by the clergyman for their interviews. The Padre was a small man, with the quick, penetrating black eyes of the Sicilian, and the superfluity of gesture and action in his conversation, which, while an Italian could not express himself without it, seems, until an Englishman or an American becomes used to it, so very strange. He was polite and kindly, and well educated, a devoted parish priest, and idolized by his parishioners.

"The more I see of Ginevra, amico,"

said Mainwaring, one evening, "the less I consider your conversion surprising. It was simply impossible that you could hold out against such inducements, and Catholicity came to you, as everything has in life, *couleur de rose*. But for me, there was no sweet-voiced woman, angel-like, to point my way to heaven, no vice-gerent of Christ to bless my faltering footsteps. Catholicity came to me in the weary hours of pain, and inforced itself upon my unwilling mind with a persistency which gave me no rest, day or night."

Louis looked at him and noticing again how pale and thin, drawn and haggard, the face of his friend was, could well underderstand what the struggle had been.

"I wish you could know Mr. Baine, Louis; my seeking him was Providential, for he was just the one to overcome my prejudices; few others could have done so."

"It has been a strange experience for both of us, Ed. Strange that we, so long friends and companions, inseparable almost since our boyhood, and while all went smoothly, should, when the real trials, temptations, and struggles of life have assailed us, been separated by our own foolish arrangement! I cannot tell you how often I have longed for a sight of your face, the clasp of your hand, the sound of your voice, and to know there would be no difference between us because of the great change which had taken place in me."

Both were silent for awhile, and then Mainwaring got up and paced the piazza, as was his wont, while Gwynne lay back in in his chair and watched him.

CHAPTER III.

THE lovely month of May came to the island with her wealth of sunny skies and balmy airs and flowers. The Gwynnes and Mainwaring were still there, but the former's health was now so completely restored that he was already making his plans for leaving. The little villa they had occupied, and indeed the whole island, with the simple, kindly people around them, had become very much endeared to them; still Louis felt anxious to be away. Padre Moroni was always a loved and frequent guest: he and Mainwaring had held many and long conversations upon the latter's plans. When such a complete change in all his habits and feelings comes to a man like Mainwaring, it is not easy for him to settle into the new order of things; and while Edgar felt that he could never return to his old way of life, either exteriorly or interiorly, he knew that he could not go on as he had been doing for the last two months. It was all very well as a resting and breathing spell—a sort of gathering of his powers, exhausted by the struggle he had been through, before he began the new life. But he felt that new life must be commenced before long. He had, too, so much lost time to make up, he considered, and was bewildered where to begin.

He corresponded regularly with Mr. Baine, and consulted frequently with Padre Moroni, and remembering the former's words to him on the occasion of their first interview and the first prayer he had ever said in an oratory, the idea came to him and grew upon him to dedicate himself in his regenerated existence to the Mother of God.

Accordingly, in her own lovely month, never more lovely than in that famed island, where flowers seem to spring in eternal freshness, in the little church dedicated to her honor, he made his solemn consecration of his life and fortunes to Mary Immaculate.

It was not long after this that he made up his mind as to his future course—he decided to join the Order of Jesus. The Gwynnes were not surprised when he told them of his decision, for they saw that no ordinary way of life would suit the new spirit which had been awakened within him.

"I have found my vocation at last, Louis," said Mainwaring, as they occupied their favorite post for enjoying the view of sea, with its multitudes of ships, and earth, with its old time ruins.

"And that?" queried Gwynne.

"Is in the ranks of God's soldiers who wear the livery of Ignatius of Loyola."

"A Jesuit! You have chosen a hard path, mon ami, not only from the strictness of the rule, but from the hatred, misrepresentation, and vilification of the world."

"I know; there is not an Order in the Church more belied and hated than that of the Jesuits, because the world knows that it has no stronger adversary, nor one who understands its falsehoods and hollow pretensions better, than the noble band of followers of Loyola—'the strongest rowers in the bark of Peter.'"

"It is strange to me now, though at one time it seemed all right, that blind, ignorant hatred which men bear to the very name of Catholic, let alone that of Jesuit. Some feel this so strongly, that the very expression of their faces change to deep disgust at the word; and while I wonder at them I cannot but remember myself with surprise," said Gwynne.

"And while we remember our past selves with surprise, is not the fact of our being led to see so differently a still recurring wonder? We used to have serious talks sometimes in those old days, Louis, albeit we were little given to taking thought for the morrow, and it seems strange that not all the horrors of war, the sights we witnessed in the Peninsula and the Wilderness, could have the power then to wake us from our indifference!"

"Our time had not come, Edgar, or we were too deeply sunk in the darkness of our own hearts to see the light then."

"But with me the awakening has been thorough. I often wonder at the old life I lead; though to others it seemed innocent enough, to me, now, it appears so empty. And now, having begun a new one, "impendam et expendar," and the world has no charms for me, the past is dead."

"Che sarà, sarà," replied Gwynne. "With me, too, the past is dead. I did hope once, old boy, to call you brother—to have seen you and Eleanore, the two beings I loved most on earth, one. But that hope died out some time ago, and yesterday she accepted the hand of Signor Novaro, a Roman gentleman whom we met last winter. I expect to return to the United States, I think I told you, not to remain, but to make arrangements for a permanent residence in Italy. I could not be happy again among the old scenes without the old spirit.

> 'Season and scene come back again,
> And outward things unchanged remain,
> The rest we cannot reinstate—
> Ourselves we cannot recreate—
> Nor set our souls to the same key
> Of the remembered harmony.'

Longfellow's words are very sad, but very true. But," he continued, in a cheerier tone, "I am glad you have chosen Rome for your novitiate, for next winter we shall certainly see you frequently. You can perceive yourself how much I have improved in the last two months, and if I continue to do so, I may reasonably hope to make the Eternal City my future home."

"That would indeed be pleasant. But I should think you would hardly be able to tear yourself away from this lovely spot, even to live under the shadow of St. Peter's. Certainly there never was a more heavenly seclusion than this island during the month of May."

"Very true, Ed., only I have a Napoleon-at-Saint-Helena sort of feeling when I look out over the sea; and when I watch the vessels sailing past my perch, I think sometimes I must fly—that I cannot breathe caged up in this little dot of earth and rock."

"And it is just the place of all others I should have thought would have suited your *far niente* disposition. However, we all change our feelings some time. I could spend the rest of my days here in perfect satisfaction but for the voice that calls me to the battle-field."

To Mainwaring, the step he was about to take seemed the only natural conclusion to all that had gone before—the only means of attaining true peace. The severity of the discipline, the setting himself apart from all earthly ties, had no terror for him. His mind had been in such a state of confusion and distress, that it had told upon his physical organization.

Naturally robust, and disciplined above all by his four years' experience in the army, as well as by the athletic sports and exercises in which he delighted, he was little in the habit of thinking of his health; but the mental strain had been so great and so long that he could not recover from it readily. He felt there was a great change, but he parried all Gwynne's allusions to it and never reverted to it himself. Still the consciousness of it made him anxious to be clothed in the blessed habit—to die, if he was to die, beneath the shelter of the noblest, grandest, and holiest of the Orders of the Church.

But he had promised his uncle to return to Boston before deciding upon his future, or, rather, before putting his decision into action, and he meant to keep his word. He dreaded the meeting and the arguments which he knew he would have to combat, by which they would seek to turn him from his course, particularly when they should discover that it was to the Order of Jesuits, that *bête noir* of Protestant imagination, his vocation had led him. To be a Catholic was terrible enough—but to be a Jesuit! What more horrible fate could an enlightened Protestant conceive of!

CHAPTER IV.

WHEN tired of exploring the island, Gwynne's yacht still lying in the harbor, they had varied their pleasures by short sails around it; in this way they had a sea view of Etna and also of Palermo.

One day Gwynne made a proposition to Mainwaring to join them in a yachting excursion which he and Ginevra had long been planning. It was now June, and, after nearly five months' stay upon the island, Louis was completely restored to his former vigor. The summer heats were becoming very intense and, to one not used to the climate, almost unbearable. His proposition was to spend a few weeks in the yacht before they sailed for the United States, as they had arranged to do together. Although it would delay his final arrangements some time, Edgar felt that he could not deny himself and refuse his friends the pleasure they so anxiously wished him to share with them.

One duty, and a very sad one, Gwynne felt was paramount over all pleasure, as soon as he was in a condition to fulfil it, and that called him to Marseilles to visit his father's grave, see in what condition it was, and erect a suitable monument to his memory. This he proposed to do before anything else.

Accordingly, about the middle of June, the Sicilian villa was given up and farewell said to their few acquaintances high and low. Padre Moroni went with them on board the yacht and remained till the hour for starting arrived, and after they had set sail he stood on the shore and waved his handkerchief until he could distinguish no form upon the deck.

The sacred and sad duty performed at Marseilles, our little party turned their course eastward, and running down past Sardinia and Sicily's southern coast, without stopping at Girgenti, their first halt was at Malta. Here they lingered two or three weeks, unable to tear themselves away from the attractions of the place; visiting the scenes made so interesting by the noble Knights of St. John before the spirit and corruption of the world destroyed their usefulness and brought about their destruction as an Order.

Thence to Alexandria, that perfect pandemonium of Eastern dialects and sects.

From Alexandria they went to Joppa, and sending the yacht on to await them at Acre, decided to visit the Holy City and its sacred surroundings.

Unspeakable to Mainwaring was the blessedness of this privilege of standing where his Lord had stood, of going up and down the same streets, meditating in Gethsemane, praying on the Mount of Olives, and kneeling in wrapt adoration upon Calvary. To the Gwynnes the enjoyment was of a different nature. But the heat of July and August was so great, they were forced to shorten their stay, and after a visit to Nazareth, where He " was subject to them," they were glad to get on board the yacht once more and leave behind them the blue Syrian skies, from which the sun shone with such intensity.

Their next stopping place was Rhodes. Here, too, they spent several days, so interested were they, in spite of the heat, in the antiquities and history of the island. Then around the Greek Peninsula and up the Dalmatian coast, with the densely-wooded peaks of the Julian Alps overhanging the shore. Stopping at Triest for a couple of days, in order to make an excursion into the neighboring country, they finally found themselves at Venice.

Around no place perhaps, after the "City of the Cæsars," do such varied and romantic memories of worldly grandeur cluster—no spot on earth is more sadly mournful in its fall than this.

"A thousand years their cloudy wings expand
    Around me, and a dying glory smiles
O'er the far times, when many a subject land
    Look'd to the winged Leon's marble piles,
When Venice sat in state, throned in her hundred
    isles.

She looks a sea-Cybele, fresh from ocean,
  Rising with her tiara of proud towers
At airy distance, with majestic motion,
  A ruler of the waters and their powers.
And such she was;—her daughters had their dowers
  From spoils of nations, and the exhaustless East
Pour'd in her lap all gems in sparkling showers,
  In purple was she robed, and of her feast
    Monarchs partook, and deem'd their dignity increased.

But unto us she hath a spell beyond
  Her name in story, and her long array
Of mighty shadows, whose dim forms despond
  Above the Dogeless city's vanish'd sway;
Ours is a trophy which will not decay
  With the Rialto; Shylock and the Moor
And Pierre cannot be swept or worn away,—
  The keystones of the arch! though all were o'er,
For us repeopled were the solitary shore."

Here they floated in gondolas through canals and lagoons, and standing upon the piazza beneath the shadow of the winged lions, saw the pigeons fed, revelled in the marble palaces and their treasures of art, and stood in wrapt admiration before the statue of Bianca Capella, whose wondrous beauty won for her the ducal coronet of Florence, and it was with difficulty they could make up their minds to fix a day for their departure, when it was delayed and rendered uncertain by a letter from Count Manzano.

He had not been able to leave Rome before, and now proposed to join them and accompany them on the remainder of their tour. Accordingly they wrote him in reply that they would await him there. In the course of a week he came, bringing with him Eleanore's betrothed, and now, the party being complete, they started down the coast of Italy.

At Marseilles again they left the yacht in the care of the sailing-master and crew, and crossing France, sailed the first of October for New York from Havre.

At New York they parted with Mainwaring, who lost no time in getting to Boston, while the others turned their faces westward.

Gwynne's fears with reference to his reception by his old acquaintances were proved true. He was looked upon with pity by some and aversion by others, and coolness by all. Even Ginevra's beauty made no difference—"the trail of the serpent was over them all." On the other hand, in the one or two Catholic families whom he had known slightly before he went away he found warm and sincere friends, to whom he felt drawn by no ordinary ties, and by them he was drawn into the sphere of their Archbishop's influence, and knowing him well, he could not but love where he had before been forced to respect. Still the change was painful to him, and he longed to be away again, to be free once more, in Papal Rome.

Mainwaring found a warm, though sad, welcome awaiting him in Boston. His uncle had never been a member of any Church, and while he considered himself free from prejudices and willing to allow everyone freedom of thought and choice, the idea of his nephew, who had been to him as a son, becoming a Catholic was a great trouble to him. He knew nothing about the Church, had never read any controversial works, but,

without seeking, much of the current abuse
and many of the lies with which the literature of the day, and New England literature
in particular, is flooded, had come to his
hand, and he had read them. Thus, while
he felt there was another side to be heard,
and, using his common sense and judgment,
looked around him at the fruits of the
Church's teachings, and found them far different from what they were represented, still
there was, unconsciously to him, a leaven
of suspicion, of distrust, and, consequently,
of dislike to the religion Edgar had chosen.

But, after finding that Edgar's decision
was not one hastily made, that he was con-
scientious in his choice, and satisfied that no
other life would content the new craving of
his soul, he did not attempt to argue with
him, or to work upon his affection for himself,
only in his heart of hearts he regretted the
in his opinion, "mistaken" kindness which
had induced him to send Edgar to Europe,
not taking into consideration that the God
who had called his nephew would have

found means to influence him here at home as readily as He did in England.

But the physical change in Mainwaring distressed his uncle still more than the religious one. Having parted from him in robust health little over a year before, he was not prepared to find him looking so very much altered. As Edgar did not refer to his state of health in any way himself, his uncle forbore to do so, but it was with a heavy heart and a conviction that he would never see him again that he bade him farewell when the time for parting came.

It was not until the spring of 1869 that Gwynne was able to complete his final arrangements for leaving his native land for ever. Count Manzano, unused to the peculiar idiosyncracies of our climate, was glad to return to his Roman skies before Christmas, but Novaro, interested in the new country and ways of living, besides having Eleanore's society to make up for other inconveniencies, remained until the Gwynnes were ready to go.

They sailed from Boston this time for Liverpool, and passing directly through England, soon found themselves on French soil. It was May before they reached Rome, and the summer of that warm latitude was upon them.

It would be impossible to describe the sentiments with which Mainwaring approached the Eternal City—the goal of all his hopes—the hallowed spot within whose walls he hoped to end his days. Nor will I attempt to describe the impression which a personal interview with the Pope made upon him. He had been accustomed to think of Pius IX as a kindly-intentioned, but weak, old man, who, in the early part of his reign, having attempted to walk hand in hand with the party of progress, and finding the influence of the Jesuits too strong—that he must lose his tiara, or keep it by following in the footsteps of his predecessors—had contentedly sunk down into the rut and gone on calmly in the old way of priestcraft, of which the liberal world was getting so weary.

He had considered him a sort of Louis XVI, the innocent scapegoat for the sins of all the Popes since Leo X, to go no further back, and since his conversion he had much wondered what manner of man he was.

Mainwaring was most anxious to begin his novitiate at once and put himself immediately into the hands of the Superior, but Gwynne pleaded with him to take no decided step until the cool weather—to come with them to Switzerland until the intense heat was over. Mainwaring resisted his friend's prayer for a long time, and turned a deaf ear to the advice of others. He knew his health was failing, and he was most anxious to complete his intention—his life, as it were —before he ended it.

But, in his frail condition, the heats of a Roman summer, together with the efforts he would have made to comply with the rules of the Order, would have soon put an end to all his worldly hopes. Fortunately, Ginevra, happening to speak to Father Beckx, the Superior of the Jesuits, about

Mainwaring and their anxiety about him, the gentleman soon saw how well grounded their fears were, and laid it upon his young would-be novice, as a test of obedience, that he give up all idea of remaining in Rome during the hot weather.

In the fervor of his wish to do everything in the proper spirit, Mainwaring made no further question, but submitted. And so Gwynne had him to himself for another six months, and together they explored the hills and valleys, lakes and mountains of romantic Switzerland.

PART FIFTH.

Rome. 1869-'71.

CHAPTER I.

LOUIS GWYNNE'S JOURNAL RESUMED.

ROME, December 10th, 1869.

THE city is filled with crowds of strangers from all parts of the world—patriarchs and archbishops, bishops, abbots, and priests—all coming at the summons of the grand old man who has filled St. Peter's chair, through suffering and calumny, so gloriously, for two-and-twenty years.

May he live to see the "years of Peter!"

And so the Ecumenical Council has met in spite of the predictions (where the wish was father to the thought) of the enemies of the Church, that the spirit of "Reform" and "Liberty and Progress" was too strong, even in down-trodden Italy, to allow the "mummeries and priestly imposition of a miserable and degraded clergy to impose upon the people any longer." It has met, to the confusion of the false prophets.

And its deliberations have gone steadily on, notwithstanding the wonderful stories which have filled the Protestant papers of quarrels and disputes and expulsions, etc.

The preparations for the Council were all fortunately completed in time. The partition which separates the portion of St. Peter's set off for the hall of the Council extends only to the arch of the transept, and does not exceed two-thirds of the heights of the pillars. It is very solid and is covered with thick linen.

A large door is in the middle, which will be open during the public sessions of the Council. In the background of the enclosed space, the seats of the Cardinals are arranged in a semi-circle, and raised seven steps above the floor of the Chapel of SS. Processus and Martinien.

The throne for the Holy Father is in the

centre, and is exalted four steps higher. Behind the throne is a passage, connected by a corridor and private staircase with the Vatican, through which his Holiness can reach it without traversing the open space.

About thirteen feet above the seats of the Sacred College are two desks in which twelve people can be easily accommodated, and these are for stenographers.

Above these desks are a row of twenty-four medallions, representing the Popes who have convened Councils. The seats of the bishops proceed in straight files from those of the Cardinals, along each side of the semi-circle. They are in six rows, each one higher than the one in front. Above these seats are two desks for the theologians, which fill up the breadth of two arcades of the right lateral nave.

The tribune for orators is at a short distance from the Pontifical throne, near the cardinals' seats; and the patriarchs are placed immediately below them.

Watchmen are kept day and night to prevent the "Party of Action," which is the polite name given to the *misèrables* who acknowledge Garibaldi and Mazzini for their leaders, from fulfilling their threats to burn down the newly-erected woodwork.

The venerable prelates who have responded to the call of the Vicar of Christ have been provided with accommodations in the various monasteries and religious houses, besides several private residences. Count Manzano has put a large portion of his palazzo at the service of the visitors. Prince Alexander Toilonia has placed at the disposal of the Pope, for the bishops, the grand and splendid palace built by Raphael, opposite the Church of Scossacavalli, which is only a few steps from St. Peter's. Prince Borghese and Prince Massino della Colonne have also opened their palaces to the venerable guests. Among the many strangers in Rome are some who in the old days called me friend. They are a little uncertain as to how to govern their conduct towards me; however, I see very little of them. Of all those coming from my old home, no one was more welcomed than its beloved archbishop.

JANUARY 12th, 1870.—The winter is passing quietly for me, for Ginevra's health is such that I do not care to leave her often. Mainwaring is very fervent in his novitiate; so much so, that Father Beckx is obliged to relax many of the rules for him, and forbid his fasting and restrain his desire for mortification. He obeys reluctantly, saying to me one day:

"How can I conquer in the sign of the cross if I am not to bear even its shadow?"

But he is very frail, and I doubt not the cross will be laid upon him at its full weight before the end.

FEB. 1st.—Mainwaring is failing very fast. I fear the earthly part of my friend will be lost to me before many weeks; our spirts who can separate?.

MARCH 16th.—Mainwaring is dead.

I have written the words, but I cannot feel them true. I closed his eyes with my own hand; yet, as I gazed upon the marble features, I could not believe they would never more respond to word or look of mine. I crossed the poor, thin hands upon his breast and laid the crucifix upon them, but I cannot feel that they will never again clasp mine in love and friendship. Oh, Edgar! Edgar! true friend, tried brother, how can I do without you?

He won his crown through patience and much suffering. May we who are left so live as to rejoin him when it will be our turn to journey to that "undiscovered country from whose bourne no traveler returns."

He was perfectly conscious all through his illness, and, though at times his sufferings were excruciating, he bore all with heavenly patience, perfect faith, and lively charity.

By the kind permission of Father Beckx, I was allowed to be much of the time, during the last days, with him; and the beauty of his character, in all the years of our intimacy, never was so thoroughly revealed to me.

A crucifix hung at the foot of the bed, and his eyes were constantly turned towards the image of his suffering Saviour.

When in great agony, upon my asking him what I should do to relieve him, he signed to the crucifix, and whispered:

"Nothing could relieve Him during the three hours He hung there; ought *I* to ask for more?"

He knew that he was dying, and expressed no fear, no regret, except that the great happiness of offering the Divine Sacrifice at least once in his life should not be his. Many loving messages, too, he sent through me to his uncle.

"And you will miss me, amico, I know," he said once; "but, old friend, let it comfort you that your love and fellowship has been very precious to me, and has thrown a halo of happiness around many an hour which would otherwise have been dark and sad."

So he has gone, ripe, to his reward. The Church has lost a devoted son, while heaven has gained another saint.

The Superior has had his remains removed from the Novitiate on the Quirinal Hill and laid before the beautiful altar of the Chapel of St. Ignatius in the Church of the Gesu. There I have just left him, awaiting the last offices of the Church. Only the full moon stealing softly through the stained-glass windows, throwing strange, faint arabesques on the floor, and the tall candles burning each side the bier, was the light in the noble building, obscuring, but not concealing, the architectural beauties and the exquisite groups, each side of the altar, of Religion destroying heresy with a cross and Faith adored by barbarous nations.

How little I thought when I went with him on his first visit to this church, and admired with him the design of Vignoli, so well carried out by Cardinal Alessandro Farnese, in 1575, with the cupola by della Porta, and stood beneath the Corinthian portico, that so soon he would be carried there—dead. Particularly was he attracted by this Chapel of St. Ignatius. Over the altar is a statue of the saint kneeling; four columns support the altar of lapis-lazuli and gilt bronze. In the middle of the pediment is a group, by Ludoise, in white marble, of the Trinity, while on either side are the groups of Faith and Religion.

It seemed strange to leave what was once almost a part of myself, lying there in "cold obstruction," with the moonlight falling on the pale, dead face, and the hands at rest forever more. I laid a cross of white flowers on his breast, they were a fit emblem of him, and in *that sign* he *had* conquered. But his feet, not his head, were turned towards the altar—the last wish of his heart was not gratified—he did not receive the crowning glory of the priesthood.

MARCH 25th.—In conversing, a few days ago, with the Superior, Father Beckx, at the Gèsu, about my dear Edgar, the Reverend gentleman pronounced a warm eulogy upon his many virtues, and said he never had seen so signal an instance of the direct guiding of the finger of God, as in his conversion and determination to devote himself to the service of the Almighty in the Order of Jesus.

"He would have been a successful missionary, for he had the gift of most persuasive eloquence in all that goes to make up the gift; a ready flow of words, a quick application, a graceful manner, an exceedingly clear, penetrating, withal sweet voice, and an earnest persuasiveness arising from his own strong faith, which few could have resisted. Had he been sent back to his old home in the United States, I should have expected most wonderful results, but," he added, with a smile, "we have lost Boston for the next twenty years."

And I, how can I do without you, Edgar? Your ready sympathy whether for joy or sorrow. Ah, amico! how can I do without you, my *alter ego*. How forego the help of your counsel and assistance, my wise Mentor!

CHAPTER II.

MAY 3d.

I MISS the clasp of my friend's hand, but I have the clutchings of a baby's pink fingers around my own! My baby boy! And my friend not here to share my happiness!

I had hoped he would have stood sponsor to the little pilgrim: placed under his guidance the young soul could not have gone astray, and now, the burden of responsibility is all mine and his mother's, with no calm, impartial judgment to rely upon. I tremble when I look at the atom the nurse and Ginevra handle so carefully, and think of what the coming years may bring to it and to me through it.

JUNE 27th. The warm weather finds us all well, but preparing for a flight to the mountains as soon as Ginevra thinks she is ready. Eleanore was married the second week in the present month, and is awaiting us " on the margin of fair Zurick's waters," having been to Paris, London, and Edinburgh on her bridal tour.

ZURICH, July 30th.—I have written nothing since we left Rome, because we were living so quietly and retired, there was no daily occurrence worth chronicling. But, now, this sad war, so suddenly opened upon us by the declaration of the 15th, makes us feel that we must be prepared for anything.

I was sorry to miss the solemn proclamation of the doctrine of Papal Infallibility at Rome on the 18th. The dogma was defined on the 13th, in the Council, by a vote of 450 to 88.

On the 17th of July, a Prussian force marched upon French territory towards Metz, and since then the ball has rolled steadily on. I am anxious to get back to Rome, though Count Manzano writes that all is still quiet there, and there is no fear of the withdrawal of the French troops.

If there is any danger, of course the sessions of the Council will be stopped, and the foreign Bishops allowed to return to their homes. The Papal Infallibility is decided upon, and "the cause is finished, Rome has spoken." "Human knowledge bows to Divine revelation," and faith will record, in the submission of all doubters, to the dictation of the Holy Spirit, victories unseen, but never to be forgotten. The debates by which the truth has been revealed have been excessively sharp, but let us hope that the unity of faith will heal all unkindness.

By those outside the Church, no doctrine has been so maliciously misinterpreted, more grossly misunderstood. The world will, and may oppose it, unavailingly. The Spirit of God has spoken, it cannot contradict itself.

August 8th.—The papers are still filled with the accounts of battles and defeats, and to a looker-on from afar, the reports are very conflicting. Each side claims the victory, and one knows not which to believe. There is now more talk of removing the French troops from Rome, and the Italian army has been nearly doubled. I think we will return to the Eternal City by the 1st of September. I am very impatient at being away.

August 26th.—"Unmerciful disaster follows fast, and follows faster" the unfortunate French army. I cannot understand the cause.

Rome, Sept. 1st.—Arrived at home safely, yesterday.

Sept. 8th.—A week of fearful and overwhelming defeats ended in the capture of Louis Napoleon, McMahon, and his whole army at Sedan. The news is so terrible that I can scarcely believe it; yet, it is true, and in it we can see the hand of God to punish the French Emperor for his forgetfulness of his duty to the Holy Father. But *France* is not conquered yet, nor will be without so fierce a struggle that the victors will rue their victory for many a day to come.

And now, "Il Re gentilhuomo" proves his chivalry.

Waiting quietly until France is powerless to prevent, and counting on the supineness of the other Catholic governments, he openly asserts his intention of robbing the Holy Father of his temporal possessions. And over this barefaced thieving he seeks to throw a cloak, by pretending that it is to prevent the Republicans from succeeding in their designs upon the Eternal City.

Oh, brave and noble hero of the Nineteenth Century, hail!

By the Convention of the 15th of September, 1864, Victor Emmanuel pledged himself not only to respect, but to defend the independence of the Papal dominions. Behold how the gentleman, *par excellence*, keeps his word.

Oh, most honorable and truthful Impersonation of the Spirit of the Age, hail!

And what folly all this talk about the unification of Italy is! A united Italy is an innovation which cannot last.

Victor Emmanuel nor Mazzini will succeed where the first Napoleon failed. The different States of Italy, formed by different races, will never coalesce, and Rome is nothing unless she is the Pope's.

SEPT. 18th.—Gen. Kenzler, the Papal war minister, has received the formal notice, from the thief at Florence, of his intention to occupy Rome. And not to lose any time, his gallant army is on the march.

The Pope will make little or no resistance, though the Zouaves and the Swiss Guard are clamorous for a repetition of Mentana.

Alas, for my weakened constitution, which prevents my arming in defence of the holy old man!

SEPT. 18th.—Baron Von Arnheim had

an interview with Cardona yesterday, at Monte Rotundo. Cardona consents to delay the attack on Rome twenty-four hours, the Baron hoping he could induce the Pope to yield a little. But the "*non possumus*" of the grand Pontiff is still the only reply.

SEPT. 22d.—The threat is accomplished—the Italian army has possession of Rome—and, now, we ask ourselves, what next? The 20th of September, 1870, will be a day long remembered. Only a faint resistance was made to the entrance of the Robber King's troops. The city was defended only long enough to prove to the world that it was taken by force, and not by supine submission.

Well! The Spirit of Evil and his agents in the flesh have triumphed; "the unification of Italy" is complete, and Pius IX has taken refuge beneath the bronze statue of St. Michael from the treachery of the crowned hypocrite, and Victor Emmanuel rules in Rome.

How long the Holy Father will remain

in the Castle of St. Angelo, or where he will next turn his weary steps, the future only can unfold.

It is not thought that the fortress can hold out against the modern engines of war, nor is it likely to be tested. Pio Nono is too humane and peace-loving to allow any lives to be sacrificed unnecessarily for him, and if *les misèrables*, who now hold Rome, should attempt to force the Castle, it will, doubtless, be yielded without resistance.

How sad must be the meditations of the thrice venerable Pontiff, as he looks out over his poor city, in the power of the worst of her children, and spirits like to themselves. In the words of Him whose Vicar he is, he can exclaim:

"*If thou also hadst known, and that in this thy day, the things that are for thy peace, but now they are hidden from thy eyes. For the days shall come upon thee, and thy enemies shall cast a trench about thee, and shall compass thee round, and straighten thee in every way. Because thou hadst not known the time of thy visitation.*"

CHAPTER III.

OCTOBER 3d.

THE last act of the farce is over. And the end was worthy of the beginning. Ever since the day the gigantic theft was perpetrated, the "glorious" 20th of September, the thieves have been preparing for their grand *coup*.

From far and near have been collected the scum of the Italian populace, with a few sprinklings of German and French. Boys of sixteen and eighteen; old men of sixty and eighty; perjured priests and renegade monks; criminals of all grades and kinds, the offscourings of the prisons, among them some of the very men whom Pius IX signalized his reign by liberating —anybody, everybody, no matter how degraded or wicked, who would blindly throw up their hats (if they possessed them) and shout for " Liberta," " Progresso," and "viva Garibaldi," or "Vittore Emmanuele," no matter how little or how much they knew of the meaning of the words. All these, and many more of the same genus, have been swarming through the Roman streets, making day unsafe, and night hideous by their proceedings, and rendering it impossible almost for any decent person to step beyond the threshold.

And yesterday, Sunday, these canaille united with their congenial spirits among the native Romans, to do the work they were brought here to do. The polls were opened, and the soldiers of the crowned thief kept watch and ward around them. All day long the voting went on, and in the evening the result was known. Rome had, by an immense majority, voted herself a part of the Italian kingdom! The City of the Cæsars, the once mistress of the Pagan—until now, the mistress of the Christian—world, contents to vote herself the slave of a petty king, whom, yesterday, the world knew not. Thus, without their wishes being allowed expression, overpowered by these tools of Satan, the Roman people are bartered away to a wretched libertine, whose ambition has blinded him, not only to all sense of decency, but to his own best interests.

After all, what has been gained? What is Rome without the Pope? Nothing but a second rate town on the banks of the Tiber.

The angels who have delivered her from her "bondage," are eager for the removal of the Italian government here.

But they are not all fools in Florence, and that result is a long way off. Victor Emmanuel will not dare take such a step, however, he may talk about it, in order to keep his precious crew quiet.

Now that the hour of bitterness and woe has come over the Head of the Church, its enemies wax strong in their fancied security.

Unwilling to profit by past experience, and acknowledging no other God but the prince of this world, they think that now

France being, for the time, powerless (and Austria indifferent) to keep the Italian ruffians at bay, the end of the Church has come.

Let them open their Bibles, which the world claims it has been the proud privilege of the present Godless crew to have rendered accessible to the poor Romans—let them read there:

"Upon this rock I will build my Church, and the *gates of hell* shall *not* prevail against it.

"*Heaven and earth* shall pass away, but my word shall *not* pass away!"

While God's word stands, so long will His Church stand. We need not heed the gibes of those who scorn us, nor the threats of those who fear us.

Oct. 10.—Cardinal Matteo, President of the College of Cardinals, is dead. Cardinal Patrizzi succeeds him.

The Florentine government has issued a decree, annexing the Roman provinces to the kingdom of Italy. The Pope is to preserve *his dignity*, and the *inviolability* of his *personal* prerogatives *as a sovereign*. Laws are promised settling the *independence* territorially of the *spiritual authority* of his Holiness!

Could the sublimity of impudence go further!

General La Marmora is appointed Lieutenant Governor of the Papal provinces, and the laws of Italy are to be introduced, and amnesty proclaimed.

Oct. 11th.—General Marmora entered Rome to-day. Of course, he made a speech. It is wonderful how much these men have to say for themselves. Victor Emmanuel has been speechifying also, in Florence. Gen. M. *hopes* the Pope will exercise *his rights* with *freedom*. And the gallant King promises, "*Liberty to the Church*, unity to Italy, and *independence to the Pontiff*."

The English saluted the Italian flag at Civita Vecchia the other day.

The "government" at Florence has decided to consolidate the Roman provinces into five prefectures. They have also fixed upon the 15th of June, 1871, as the day upon which the "government" will be removed to Rome. But the Roman nor the Catholic world need be alarmed: the 15th of June will come and go, and the "government" will stay where it is.

Our domestic matters are going on as smoothly as possible. The baby don't sneeze any more frequently than is natural, and shuts his eyes when he goes to sleep, and draws his rations regularly; all of which is very satisfactory to Ginevra and her father.

But day by day I miss Edgar's friendship and companionship more and more. No one can take *his* place.

Meantime the siege of Paris progresses, and God only knows what He has in store for that lovely city.

Oct. 20th.—The interview between the Cardinal Secretary of State and the Embassador of Victor Emmanuel, Count Ponza, only reveals the fact that no reliance can be placed upon any assurance of personal liberty of action that has been made to the Holy See. The spiritual independence of the Church will perish if left to the protection of the atheists of the Italian Parliament.

The present "possession" of Rome is as diabolical as any recorded of men or women in Sacred Writ! The city is rapidly being converted into a den of thieves. The progressive Garibaldians and their dear friends the banditti have given us a taste of what we are to receive from the government which is to supercede the rule of Pius IX. The prisons have been thrown open indiscriminately and the worst wretches turned loose upon us. Churches are desecrated and convents sacked every day.

I do not allow Ginevra to go outside the garden walls, and even there she is not always safe. Count Manzano being well known as a devoted adherent of the Pope, his house is a special object of attention, and as the garden can be overlooked from neighboring houses, my wife's daily walk has once or twice been rendered rather unpleasant. The attacks have been, so far, only wordy ones, but we know not how soon they may be followed up by other missiles. The pistol and stilletto are now the order of the day!

And this is Liberty!

For Catholics the question of the hour is very solemn and momentous. It is not a mere political question—the defeat of this or that party; it is not a mere local question, or that of material interest; it is the question of the authority and independence of the Holy See. And it is not a question merely of the independence of the Pope himself, or of the people of the diocese of Rome, or of the Italian kingdom—it affects the spiritual welfare and eternal destiny of every Christian soul living and of the millions that are yet to come. Rome is the source of all ecclesiastical authority:

cut off the source of that and it is unnecessary to draw a picture of the evils that will follow. To seal up this fountain is to cut off the souls of men from heaven.

Nov. 12th.—Count Manzano is very ill. One day last week, while ascending the steps at the Trinita dei Monte, he was set upon by a couple of ruffians, who were half tipsy. They had an old red flannel cap, which they attempted to force upon the Count's head, and ordered him to shout "Viva liberta e Vittore Emmanuele." He was pretty severely handled before the accidental appearance of several ex-Zouaves, who happened still to be in Rome, put his tormentors to flight. This, with his anxiety for the Holy Father and his distress at the horrors which have been brought upon Rome by her "liberators," which produced a low nervous fever, under which he has been struggling for several weeks, has finally prostrated him.

The English and American papers are filled with the most highly-colored accounts of the enthusiasm with which the "people" of Rome welcomed the soldiers of the Robber-King. It is a well-known fact that, of the forty thousand majority which gave Rome to Victor Emmanuel, two-thirds were the offscouring and scum of other Italian cities, and the remaining one-third was made up of the most ignorant, credulous, and debased portion of the Roman populace. The educated and intelligent Romans were loyal beyond expression. They refused, to a man, to vote. They freely volunteered to serve the Pope, and the Palatine Guard, of which Eleanore's husband was a member, composed of the first blood in the city—princes and barons and counts serving in the ranks—defended the western part of the city, and stood firm under a six hours' deadly fire from the guns of their "deliverers." Rather a peculiar welcome, and a new manner of showing dislike to the Papal rule.

The Zouaves, hiding away in the houses of the inhabitants to escape the fury of the mob, were concealed faithfully, and not one betrayed.

When may anything relating to Catholicity hope for truth or justice?

Of all the sad and touching sights which I have witnessed, nothing was more moving than the farewell of the Zouaves to the Holy Father, after they were disbanded and as they marched out of the city. The Pope stood at a certain window in the Vatican (to which he has returned from Castle St. Angelo) which had been privately indicated to them; and as the little band of brave and devoted soldiers came to that part of the street from which they could see the window, every bared head was turned and bowed for an instant for the unseen, though not unfelt, benediction.

CHAPTER IV.

February 14th, 1871.

I HAVE been too much occupied with my father-in-law's illness, too much distressed by the state of things around me, to care to take note of them. But now we are in the midst of the Carnival and its glories must be duly chronicled.

The King of Italy made his entrance into the city he so bravely acquired last September on the 31st of December. Of course his friends were rejoiced to see him, and a grand illumination and riot at night were the means they chose to express their joy. And equally, of course, no one who valued his life, or had the least regard for decency, would venture into the streets. But we ought not to blame them too severely, for if thieves and cut-throats are ever to rejoice with impunity and practice their calling freely it surely will be under the patronage and in order to do honor to their KING.

Yesterday the Commission visited the Convents of the Minerva and Silvestrines, the Collegio Romano and that of Monte Citorio; the Fathers of the Mission have been ordered to depart from the latter building, their lawful home and possession, in sixteen days, the thieves having designed it for the Chamber of Deputies. The others named are to be cleared by the end of April. The Casanatese Library at the Minerva and the Museum of the Roman College are to be retained, as of public utility.

The Piedmontese princes are here, and there is some discussion about their chaplain having been forbidden to say Mass in the Pauline Chapel at the Quirinal, which palace has been appropriated for the royal residence. I have not enquired into the facts of the case, nor do I feel any interest in them.

On the 12th, day before yesterday, the Scala Santa was a second time profaned. Three men with cigars in their mouths and hats on attempted to walk up: two succeeded; the third was caught by the foot, dragged down, and kicked out into the street by a Roman.

As for the murders, they have become so frequent as to excite no comment. Shamed into some show of decency, the new régime has ordered that all drinking saloons must be closed at 10 P. M. from September to February, and at 11 P. M. from March to September. Coffee houses are allowed to open one hour before daylight and must close at midnight in summer and at 11 o'clock in winter. Eating houses are to open at 8 A. A. and close at midnight at all seasons. The same rule applies to billiard saloons and other gaming houses.

This decree of the Giunto has given great offence, it being considered merely a means of extorting money.

In one of these coffee houses, in the Via del Aqua Santa, a few days ago, a letter-carrier was murdered by a man who owed him the paltry sum of twenty-five cents.

Yesterday the Corso was quite animated.

The Princess Margharita enjoyed the scene from her balcony at the Hotel de Rome. She is a sweet-faced, delicate-looking woman; her beauty a little disfigured, perhaps, by a gôitre, which she partially covers with a broad velvet ribbon. Her golden hair is almost as luxuriant as Ginevra's. But there is an intense sadness of expression in her face and smile which is touching, and she has the appearance of acting a part by no means congenial, and of being far superior to her fat, awkward lout of a husband.

Notwithstanding the vaunted enthusiasm for the Carnival, almost the whole garrison, is under arms in and near the Corso, while the Pizzareloni, the Agents of Public Safety, and the National Guard are all on duty.

Sometimes, however, our "deliverers" find themselves outwitted. Last Saturday, a man went into a wine shop and asked for a drink. The proprietor was absent, and as he seated himself, the *misèrable* ordered the waiter to extinguish the three lights burning before "that *pupazza*," indicating the statue of the Blessed Virgin over the entrance. The waiter refused to obey his order, when the man performed the meritorious action himself.

On the proprietor's return, he immediately demanded to know who or what had caused the unwonted dishonor to the Madonna. The delinquent being pointed out to him, he seized a wax taper in one hand and in the other a huge knife and forced the "patriot" to relight the three tapers, and then drove him from the door.

One of the most outrageous attacks upon the Papal Guard of the Vatican took place last Friday. Six of these Swiss, while quietly watching outside the Porta Cavalleggeri, were surrounded by quite a crowd, including the Guards of Public Safety, and searched, under the pretence of carrying arms. They were seized by twos, bound, ironed, beaten, and imprisoned until after sunset, when they were released. Of course there is no hope of obtaining satisfaction for such outrages. They must be endured with what patience their victims can command until the end.

FEB. 15th.—Yesterday the second session of the Communal Council was held, and the next session is fixed for Ash-Wednesday.

The Colosseum was illuminated last evening in the "national" colors and the arms of Savoy by Bengal lights. The princes, of course, were present.

The *Capitale* and other "liberal" papers are filled constantly with abusive and blasphemous lies about the Pope and the Church. For some time past the press has been greatly excited over an imaginary enlistment of soldiers in the cause of the Pope, and the affair has actually been carried before Parliament, where, however, it was dismissed as ridiculous. Not willing, however, to give up the idea, a grand discovery of a Papal conspiracy was made, and last Sunday an inquisitorial visit was made to the cell of Father Vannutelli, a Dominican monk and brother-in-law of General Kanzler, in the

Convent of Santa Sabina upon the Aventine. After an exhaustive search, all that rewarded their industry was a monogram of the Holy Name Jesus and some appropriate Scripture texts; also, the plan of a cross to be distributed among a Catholic Sodality called the "Soldiers of Jesus Christ—Christian Crusaders." Nevertheless, the most absurd rumors are flying about and printed in the lying liberal sheets.

FEB. 16th.—Last evening witnessed a scene which passes all description; it was one worthy of the most abandoned days of the Pagan rulers of the Eternal City, and one which Christianity, even that diluted form of it called Protestantism, ought to have rendered impossible.

The party instrumental in bringing about the search of Padre Vannutelli's cell, in order to divert from themselves the ridicule consequent upon the result, got up a masquerade, which, notwithstanding the published assurance by the powers that be, that nothing ridiculing religion would be allowed, paraded through all the streets of Rome unimpeded. It formed in the Piazza di Spagna, where Prince Humbert met the procession and cordially saluted it!

It was styled the "Crusade of 1871," and the first figure was a man dressed to resemble Peter the Hermit, riding a horse, and bearing a pair of huge manacles, a threat to the Roman people. Next came a band of music. Then a mask representing Colonel de Charette, riding a donkey, and bearing a large sabre covered with blood. After him came Swiss Squadriglierri and Zouaves, Kanzler and Zappi in their generals' uniform, the masks representing their features perfectly. There were banners with various inscriptions: "Through train for Belgium," "Crusade of '71." A dwarf bore a flag with the words: "Portæ Inferni non prævalebunt." A friar carried a fac-simile of the cross made by Padre Vannutelli, with the inscription: "Christus regnat, Christus imperat." One of the masks, a resemblance to the editor of the *Unita Cattolica*, carried a banner upon which was painted an enormous finger (the finger of God—Il Dito, as it is called), with the words "In hoc signo vinces."

How my poor Edgar's heart would have bled had he been here to witness the desecration of what he held so sacred! And if the blessed in heaven *can* feel any regret for what is done on earth, with what sorrowful eyes must not the whole hierarchy regard this sad and sacred city!

Nuns, monks, priests, bishops, cardinals, the ex-King of Naples, Cardinal Antonelli, and others, were represented. Don Pirlone Filio personated the Holy Father, giving his benediction as he passed along.

Upon a car was borne a group representing the death of "*Don Temporale*." A figure lay upon a couch and by its side stood *Don Margotto* in the act of giving the last benediction, and over his head was a scroll bearing the words "He is almost gone!" This hero had a stone thrown at him which almost stunned him, the courageous thrower of the missile eluding the guards who were formed in line to defend the masquerade.

During the march, the cries were frequent of "Death to the Pope!" "Death to the Priests!" "Down with the Jesuits!" "Death to Father Curci!" and many others.

FEB. 17th.—Yesterday being *Giovedi Grassi*, the gala day of the Carnival, the Corso swarmed with people, the *Ghetto* being well represented.

In the procession was a car draped alternately with the *American* and Italian flags at the four corners; the sides of the car were covered with the Italian colors, while in the centre was the United States shield. The *Nuova Roma*, a government organ, thus notices this fact: "Among the rest was a large car, drawn by four horses, and floating the American flag. The flags so used belonged to Messrs. W. De Lancy Ward, of New York, and R. Wilfred Blatchford, of Cincinnati. These two gentlemen were the official representatives of the American Club. We have, therefore, in a certain manner, likewise the manifest approbation of the United States. Most Eminent Antonelli, there is a fine subject for another fine note! Those two gentlemen made noise enough for forty."

It is time a stop was put to this. Our beautiful flag is dragged in the dirt on every occasion of public demonstration; it is frequently entwined with the banner of Italy. The American Consul was the only one of the foreign representatives to display his national flag on the 31st of December last, when the King made his entrance into the city.

It is galling to hear the remarks of the foreigners, particularly the English, on this act of folly; and the Italians themselves speak of it sneeringly as "*quel pezzo di straccio!*" It is the only foreign flag thus prostituted, the only one which has appeared upon the Corso during the Carnival, and the United States has the satisfaction of being the *only* foreign Power to insult the Pope in his own capital.

A crusade is being aroused against the Jesuits. The *Circolo Cavour* has issued a petition to the Parliament demanding that the laws of 1848 be extended to Rome, and the whole of the *Collegio Romano* is to be appropriated for the use of the Minister of the Interior.

Also, the museums and library of the Vatican have been declared *national property, and free right of entrance proclaimed,* although the ways and means have not been decided upon.

This afternoon an English lady was grossly insulted in passing through one of the streets adjacent to the Corso. Her offence was that she had in her hand packages of confetti done up in white and yellow papers. As she crossed the Via della Croce two *decently dressed* men assailed her, tore the packages from her and threw them into the streets, using towards her vile epithets. They also tore off her bonnet and threw it into the street, and rent her dress, besides laying violent hands on her maid, whom they insulted grossly.

Feb. 22d.—Ash-Wednesday. Quiet is at length restored, and the Lenten services have begun. The theatres, however, are not to be closed during the holy season, and the opera is at the Apollo, opening with the "Huguenots," "unscissored by Monte Citorio."

This morning the preparations for transforming the Palace of Monte Citorio, intended for the Chambers, were begun. The Senate is to be located in the Palazzo Madonna, the Minerva is appropriated for the Ministry of Finance, the Palazzo di Firenze for Foreign Affairs, the Convent of St. Agostino for the Marine, the Convent of the Eighty-eight Apostoli for War, the Piazza Colonna for Grace and Justice, the Monastery of San Sylvestro for Public Works, and the Roman College for the Ministry of the Interior.

Feb. 23d.—To-day, at the Basilica of St. Maria in Trastevere, there will be an Exposition of the Blessed Sacrament and solemn Benediction, in reparation of the sacrilege committed there several days ago by some person who broke open the tabernacle and stole the ciborium.

One of the most modern and progressive works of art yet attempted was displayed in one of the shop windows in the Corso a few days ago. It was the crucifixion. Upon the cross hung Napoleon III, the centurion piercing his side represented the King of Prussia, while the Pope and several others, representing the Apostles, stood about in most absurd attitudes of grief and dismay.

The name of the great and pious artist is not known; he ought to have a place higher than Raphael, Leonardo, and the rest.

CHAPTER V.

MARCH 10th.

I AM full of anxiety, for my precious wife is very ill.

MARCH 15th.—Ginevra is no worse, but little better. This is my dear Edgar's anniversary. I had a Mass said for him, though I feel sure his spirit, purified by its earthly sufferings, has long ago joined the ranks of those who see God face to face. Ah, amico! how can words express the longing I have felt for you during this year—how in my heart of hearts I have missed you!

APRIL 2d.—Palm Sunday. Ginevra is better—decidedly better. Thank God for all his mercies! She is out of danger. How could I have borne her loss? I shudder when I think how near she was to the portals of eternity. Her life hung by a thread, and I feared each night to see the sun rise upon her dead face. From the depths of my soul do I chant Halleluia!

April 9th.—The splendors and the solemn, majestic sadness of the Church services of Holy Thursday and Good Friday have been left to the imaginations of the people this year. St. Peter's was silent. The Pope performed all the ceremonies quietly within the closed doors of the Sistine Chapel; only a few privileged persons, besides the cardinals and higher clergy, were admitted, and I am happy to say my father-in-law and I were among the few.

Ginevra is not yet able to leave her room.

But the liberals and their Protestant friends have not been silent or quiet. On Good Friday, a *banquet* was served *in derision* of the day, and at that banquet they partook of a dish of meat moulded into the shape of our Saviour stretched upon the cross!

Could Satanic ingénuity go further? If

I had not been assured of the fact from authority unquestionable—if the demons themselves had not boasted of it—I would not have credited it. But it is true, and sometimes "truth is stranger than fiction."

A liberal paper, called the *Lampione*, filled its columns all last week with caricatures of the Passion. In one of the pictures—Veronica presenting the handkerchief—our Saviour is represented as leaving the impression of an ass' head.

So the leaven of modern liberalism and progress works its way certainly and irresistibly to the lowest and vilest corruption and the most anti-Christian horrors of infidelity.

April 17th.—The news from Paris is terrible, and the destruction of the whole city seems inevitable.

Ginevra is so much better that I carried her down into the saloon for an hour this afternoon.

The murdering of monks and priests still

goes on, and the Holy Father is obliged to submit, through his servants, to every conceivable insult. But if his heart is saddened by seeing his Eternal City in the hands of these Satanic emissaries, it must still be in some degree comforted by the addresses of sympathy and condolence which are pouring in upon him on every side.

April 19th.—The major excommunication has been pronounced against Döllinger at last. He carries a brave face now, and seems determined to throw himself heart and soul into the arms of the enemies of the Church, but the day will come when his repentance will be bitter; unless, indeed, God's grace be entirely withdrawn and he dies impenitent. Which God forbid!

May 1st.—Paris is still at the mercy of those fiends in human shape, the brothers of those who have held Rome in their toils for the last months.

It would be difficult to decide which set was the worst.

The Italian government, to give some substance to its promises of the immense good its rule was to bring to the Eternal City, have been making strenuous efforts to get the streets cleaned and demand the admiration of the world for the great benefit which they have conferred.

They have also *cleaned* the *Coliseum* of all the ivy and luxuriant vines which have clothed and consecrated its shattered walls and in a measure held them together for so many ages, thus destroying one of the most time-honored and picturesque relics of the city. Many of the old historic palaces and houses have been torn down to widen the streets, and all the world holds up its hands in admiration and delight.

But the condition of the people is fearful in spite of the lies that are written hence to the English and American papers. All schools are closed but those "allowed" by the government, and riot and murder and disorder of every shape are rampant.

Behold in Rome and Paris the accomplishment of the idea of **Progress** and **Liberty** as understood by the nineteenth century.

MAY 2d.—Our baby's birthday! The little pilgrim is one year old to-day, and so far seems to take kindly to life and its woes and duties. May he never feel the one too heavily or neglect the other.

MAY 5th.—Selfish as it may seem to leave the Holy Father to his imprisonment, I fear we cannot continue to make Rome our home. The insults and outrages are growing too frequent and great to be endured much longer.

To "give the devil his due," it is but fair to chronicle that the "government" is really trying to keep down the mob; but they might as well try to stop Niagara Falls with a feather! Like the fisherman in the "Arabian Nights," having uncorked the bottle, they cannot prevent the genie from attaining his full height.

This morning Count Manzano was again

most grossly insulted in the streets; fortunately, I happened to be riding past at the moment, and came to his assistance with a couple of *gensd'arme*.

How terrible is the condition of Paris at the mercy of the Communists; and from the news that comes to us from there, we can judge what would be the fate of Rome had not Victor Emmanuel still some sense of decency, if not fear of God, left; for the same spirit animates the two factions; they are brothers in ideas and wishes. The only difference is that while the one portion are their own masters and able to carry out their fiendish brutality unchecked, the others are restrained by the fear of going too far, and so depriving themselves of their royal tool, who, if they showed themselves in all the horrors of their true character, might be awakened to a sense of his degradation and emboldened to call for help to relieve himself of his tyrants and return to his duty as a king and a Catholic.

MAY 15th.—I want to leave Rome immediately, but Ginevra begs me so earnestly to let her remain until the Pope's Jubilee that I cannot refuse. I do not let her go out, nor will Novaro allow Eleanore to leave the precincts of his house, consequently all the communication between the families is carried on by us.

My life, taking it in strictly domestic sense (for all Catholics must feel saddened, troubled, and insulted by the state of things here), is a very happy one. My health is completely re-established. I seem to have taken a new lease of life, and the prohibition the doctor made of my resuming my military duties I regard as superfluous; could I do any good I would gladly shoulder a musket to-morrow, and feel certain I should not suffer from the exertion.

Ginevra sits beside me as I write, Luigi *secundo* in her lap serenely cheerful, knowing that at the least pucker of his baby lips, the slightest symptom of a flush rising to his infant forehead, the sure precursor of a cry, grandpa and mamma, and even aunt and uncle when able to be present, will start with anxious haste to avert the impending evil and restore his bambinoship to his usual calm complacency, while padre laughs at them for the fuss they make over the mite.

The room is the same in the Palazzo Manzano in which I had that momentous interview with Ginevra the day before the Mentana affair, during which the little woman first awoke to the consciousness that my safety, and in fact myself, were very precious in her eyes. As she bends over the babe in her lap, her golden hair flowing freely as I love to and will have it when we are alone, I can compare her to but one other picture: that of THE Mother and Child, divinely beautiful in heavenly love.

Count Manzano is never far from the boy, whose small frame in fact seems an inexhaustible magnet, drawing all the family, great and small, master and servants, to gaze and gaze and poke a finger at him or imprint a kiss upon his baby brow and go away again, only to return and repeat the performance.

So the life that is before me seems to promise much joy and happiness, and to be filled with blessings, if we so use them that no sorrow need come to teach us to be wise.

But with all this there is a vacant corner of my heart which can never be occupied, and every day "I long for the touch of a vanished hand—the sound of a voice that is still." My lost Edgar's memory never fades.

> "I cannot see the features right,
>   When on the gloom I strive to paint
>   The face I know; the lines are faint
> And mix with hollow shapes of night.
>
> Cloud towers by ghostly masons wrought,
>   A gulf that ever shuts and gapes,
>   A hand that points, and pallid shapes
> In shadowy thoroughfares of thought.
>
> And crowds that stream from yawning doors,
>   And schools of puckered faces drive;
>   Dark hulks that tremble half alive,
> And lazy lengths on boundless shores.
>
> Till all at once, beyond the will,
>   I hear a wizard music roll,
>   And through the lattice in the soul,
> Looks thy dear face and makes it still."

CHAPTER VI.

June 1st.

THERE is not much to chronicle now-a-days outside of the family except the continuous insults of every variety which are heaped upon the Pope, either through the disregard or contradiction of former regulations or in the persons of those who are devoted to his service. And of these poor Count Manzano has borne his full share. I feel anxious about him; the state of the city and the small prospect there seems of delivery for the Pope weighs upon his mind and is making him really ill. Ginevra, too, notices this, and is terribly anxious; of course I do not acknowledge to her all my fears.

Meantime the 16th approaches, and we are busy making what preparations we can. It is feared that the "liberals" will seize the opportunity of the Jubilee to get up a riot, as an excuse for further outrages.

June 8th.—All thought of rejoicing in the Papal Jubilee, or indeed of anything else, has been far from our minds for the last three days. Baby Louis has been very, very ill, and we have watched him day and night. We thought for awhile that the angels had come for him and that he would go with them, but God was merciful, and to-day a change for the better has come and the doctors say he will live. What a wealth of love those little creatures draw to themselves! all unconsciously, until some sudden danger to them show us our own hearts and how desolate we would be without them.

June 15th.—The baby is quite well again.

June 16th.—The Day! To-day Pio Nono has equalled the years of Peter, and the Jubilee began this morning. The "government" has been fearful that there would be an "uprising" in the Pope's favor; therefore, under the cloak of "keeping the peace," the streets are picketed with police, national guards, carabineers, and troops of the line, as if a Catholic army were before the walls. And the one who would be foolhardy enough to wear the white and yellow, or throw up his cap for Pio Nono, would have small chance of escape.

Minister Garda, the royal commissary, yesterday issued a proclamation to the *Romans, i. e.,* the riff-raff who have assumed to control the destinies of the city, expressing the hope that they would, *with their usual moderation and good sense, allow* the Pontifical Jubilee to pass unmolested, as a *splendid confirmation* of the *entire liberty* which religion and *its* servants *have enjoyed* and *do* en oy under the new rule!

As a corollary to this, let me add, that one or two Papal flags, which were hung out, were pounced upon by the police and confiscated. One bore the inscription "Long live Pius IX." So much for the liberty they prate of.

We were among the earliest to visit the Vatican, and received the blessing and genial greeting of the Holy Father. Eleanore was with us, and it was the first time she had seen the Pope, except in the performance of his public duties, and she was charmed, as she could not but be, by his graceful, suave manner.

Yesterday was to have been the day upon which the government of Italy was to be removed to Rome. Some time ago it was announced that the removal was postponed until July 1st. Will it be accomplished then? Perhaps so; Providence sometimes allows strange things to happen; but if it is allowed, it will not be for long.

JULY 17th.—The ecclesiastical celebration of this great Jubilee commenced in the evening of yesterday at 7 o'clock, the hour at which the Pope was elected a quarter of a century before, by the solemn exposition of the Blessed Sacrament in the Basilica of San Giovanni Laterano. This morning, High Mass was sung at the altar before the Chair of Peter. St. Peter's was gorgeously decorated and filled with devout worshipers, but of course the pomp and show of the military element was conspicuously wanting.

Yesterday, at an early hour, the long chain of carriages from the interior of the city to the colonade of the Vatican began to move, and was kept up the whole day and is continued to-day. The "liberals" look on gloomily, and do all they can by word and gesture to insult the visitors; I hope they may go no further.

Large sums of money have been brought by the foreign deputations, as well as presents of great value. The Holy Father cannot be said to want for that for which all the world is striving; he must have several millions of francs in his coffers.

A company of Italian police and soldiers guard the entrance to the Vatican, but at the entrance to the staircase leading to the Pope's apartments a large number of Swiss Guards and sergeants-de-ville stand.

No one is allowed to enter who has not or cannot produce the permit to do so, and all who are thought to have any sympathy with the Robber King and his cause are carefully excluded.

Any illumination of the city to-night has been forbidden by the authorities.

Among the preparations made for the day, by the Roman nobility, was a medal struck in commemoration. Several duplicates in gold have been given to the Pope, two hundred in silver were distributed, and I was fortunate enough to get one; besides, several in bronze have been cast, and after that the mould was broken.

The Catholics of Rome presented a jewelled clasp for a cope; another association offered a golden chalice with five thousand dollars; the Belgian Catholics offered a triple crown, enriched with jewels; Monsignor Sayazani, of Naples, offered a diamond pin worth thirty-five thousand dollars.

A new canopy of bronze, like the baldachino over the grand altar of St. Peter's, has been erected over the bronze statue of St. Peter, and was unveiled yesterday afternoon, and revealed in the front a medallion portrait of the Pope, supported by two gilt angels, with this inscription beneath it:

Pio IX. Pont. Max.
Qui Petri annos
In Pontificatu Romano
Unus Aequavit,
Clerus Vaticanus
Sacram Ornant Sedem.
XVI Kal. Quint. AMDCCLXXI.

The likeness is very good. The painted medallion is only temporary, a similar one in bronze is to be executed.

Not one of the reigning sovereigns, not even excepting Queen Victoria, failed to send their congratulations. Victor Emmanuel had the impudence to offer his also, but Cardinal Antonelli was firm in his refusal to admit the envoy.

Well, the spell is broken! It has been reserved for the 19th century to witness the first repetition of the "years of Peter" in the unbroken chain of Pontiffs for eighteen hundred years; but if the Red Revolutionists could have had their way the day would have been a bloody one. The secret of their diabolical plot is out. They had made every arrangement for the assassination of the Holy Father. Having murdered the gentle and saintly Archbishop Darboy, they thirsted for higher, though there could be no holier, blood. For obvious reasons the details have been suppressed by the Florentine government, but the main facts have leaked out in spite of them. The day fixed upon was Friday, June 16th; the place, one of the corridors of the Vatican. All this was arranged in meetings of the International Society in Paris, London, and Florence, and the agents of the deed of darkness were sent to Rome in different disguises, and by different routes. The first design of doing the murder in one of the corridors was abandoned because of some difficulty, but it was confidently expected that it could be done on Sunday while the Pope would be on his way to say Mass in the Sistine Chapel.

So complete were all the arrangements, and so confident were the assassins of success, that they boasted of it openly, and offered to bet that three days after the 16th the Pope would be dead! But their "vaulting ambition o'erleaped itself, and fell on the other side." By this very overweening security their secret was discovered.

The men have been arrested, and are still held in durance, perhaps to remain so for some time, but it is not at all likely that they will be brought to trial. The mere fact of such a conspiracy having been set on foot will not tend to make the new order of things more popular, and so the affair will be hushed up.

And suppose they had succeeded? Death can have no terrors for a soul like Pius IX's. He would welcome it as the greatest mercy his enemies could do him. In the course of his long and checkered, and yet glorious reign, he has had heavy lessons of the ingratitude of mankind, and remembering the saying of Adrian IV, can most heartily endorse it: "The chair of Peter is the most uneasy seat in the world."

June 17th. The Jubilee still continues, and the city is as quiet as its mob-masters will allow it to be. The government was most anxious to prevent the foreign deputations from suffering annoyance, as it is of primary importance that these foreign visitors should be gulled into believing the Pope to be free to do and to go what and where he pleases, in spite of his protests to the contrary.

The result has been that no general outbreak has taken place, although the hordes of Communists and Internationalists can not be perfectly controlled, infesting, as they do, the streets of our beautiful city, and making themselves the terror of its peaceful inhabitants. A number of these fellows assembled near the gates of the Vatican, and grossly insulted the members of the different deputations as they went to present their congratulations. Other deputations were hooted at in the streets, and the Germans were so violently assaulted that they were obliged to take refuge in the convent *de l'Anima.*

So much for the "free Church in a free State," of which so much has been said.

As a further proof of the freedom of the Church since the "possession" of Rome, it should be mentioned that all religious processions have been stopped, no religious ceremonies have been allowed to be performed outside of the churches, and the Blessed Sacrament is carried privately to the sick and dying. Yes, the Church is very free, thanks to Victor Emmanuel and his fellow thieves.

In no large city of the world was this remarkable anniversary celebrated with fewer joyous manifestations and open triumph than in this, the Pope's own. Not a Papal banner was allowed to wave to proclaim to the devout pilgrim that here was, indeed, the Head of Christendom— that the city was the common inheritance of the faithful. And, while the infidel and scoffer might feel at home, and roam at will over the hallowed ground, the pious Christian is regarded as a stranger, looked upon suspiciously, and, perhaps, like the Father he has come to visit, like Him whose insignia he bears, loaded with revilings.

But if the Roman people were not permitted to get up public demonstrations, they could and did testify, by their private devotion, their loyalty to the rightful sovereign, Pius IX. And many were the *benedicites* and *evvivas* which arose to heaven, unheard by mortal ears.

June 19th.—Sunday.—The jubilee still continues and will until the 21st, the day of Pius IX's enthronement.

Although the Pope is robbed of his temporal power, he has had ample proof in the last few days that he still reigns in the hearts of millions. Rome has been filled with an immense crowd of pilgrims of all ranks, from the peer to the peasant, from every nation on the earth. But Germany, France, Belgium, Holland, and England were conspicuous in their devotion! As far as I can learn, President Grant was the only ruler of a great nation who neglected to present his congratulations, and this omission, or, to call things by their right name, want of courtesy has caused much comment among the English speaking visitors.

Quite an exciting event occurred in the Albergo d' Inghilterra this morning. The Earl of Gainsboro', who accompanied his son, Hon. Edward Noel, the leader of the deputation from the Catholic youth of England to Rome, has taken rooms in this hotel, which is in the Via Bocca di Liona, with some members of the deputation.

The hotel keeper knew perfectly well what had brought his noble visitors to the Eternal City; but, notwithstanding, during their absence at Mass this morning, and without so much as saying "by your leave," a tricolored flag was hung out of their windows, although their were sixteen other windows from which it might have been displayed.

Besides, Sunday was no national holiday, nor was there the least necessity for this display.

On his return from church, Mr. Noel withdrew the flag, which was then displayed from an upper window. A crowd soon afterwards gathered around the hotel, and the manager insisted upon its being replaced.

Upon this Mr. Noel announced that he and his party would leave the hotel if the flag were forced upon them.

Nevertheless, the tricolored rag was replaced, and before it was fastened, the manager waved it several times, upon which the crowd shouted, "Viva Vittore Emmanuele!" and Mr. Noel courageously replied, by crying, "Viva Pio Nono!"

As soon as the Earl of Gainsboro' returned, he concurred in his son's decision to leave the hotel, and so the hotel keeper had a good opportunity of weighing the costs of loyalty to the delightful new government.

CHAPTER VII.

June 25th.

MY heart sickens over the condition of things, and the records of every day are disgusting.

Our great anxiety now is for Count Manzano, who is in a most miserable condition of mind and body. The grand entry of the Robber-King into his newly-stolen city is fixed for July 3d, and great preparations are being made for it.

July 1st.—Thousands of Romans are quitting Rome to avoid being present at the ensuing rejoicings. And thousands of Victor Emmanuel's creatures are pouring into it, in order to prove to the world the delight of the "citizens" at the presence of their new sovereign. All the rag-tag and bob-tail, the scum and rabble that voted the city away last October, are again collecting to do honor to their king. During the day trains have been arriving in quick succession bearing recruits for the "*spontaneous*" rejoicing. A large number of the men wore red shirts. The government has issued tickets at half price. From the neighboring towns the companies of National Guards have been invited, and free quarters provided for them. In fact, nothing is omitted to make up for the absence of the higher and respectable class of Romans. We propose to leave the city quietly after early Mass to-morrow in our own carriage, as if for a drive, and take up our quarters in a country seat I purchased early in the spring just at the foot of the Alban hills.

The programme for the procession and celebration is as follows:

His Majesty will arrive at 12.30 to-morrow, July 2. The cortege will proceed to Piazza di Spagna, thence by the Via Condotti, Corso, the Sadioni, back to the Quirinal. The evening to be devoted to the opening of the National Shooting Gallery, the ceremonies to begin at 6 o'clock. Then a dinner of two hundred covers to be given at the Quirinal, and a representation at the Apollo theatre.

On Monday there is to be a grand reception at the Palace, a review of the National Guard at the Prati Famesina at half-past five P. M., and a ball at the capitol. General illumination, music, and fireworks in the various piazzi in the evening.

There was no illumination *allowed* at the Pope's Jubilee!

An arch of triumph has been erected at the Porto del Popolo, and a sort of amphitheatre, whence the King will witness the review. Great preparations are being made for the ball, and most strenuous efforts to ensure a large attendance.

JULY 2d.—Our departure was prevented this morning by the illness of my father-in-law, and so all we can do is to keep in the house, with windows down and blinds closed.

At Mass in the Chapel of the Blessed Sacrament in St. Peter's, while Mgr. Vitelleschi was giving Holy Communion this morning, he was interrupted and so seriously annoyed and interfered with by a party of the new masters of the city, that he was obliged to dismiss the congregation and close the church.

Lanza, Sella, Acton, Comenti, and Visconti-Venosta have arrived and taken possession of the various palazzi and monasteries which have been stolen for them.

It is thought that about forty thousand of the rag-tag and roughs who call themselves "Italian patriots" have thronged into the city in order to render his Majesty's welcome "unanimous and heartfelt," &c., &c. But the absence of the respectable, prominent, and noble Roman families is very marked, those who, like ourselves, are unable to get away keeping strictly to their houses, with closed doors and windows.

These creatures who are brought into the city to do the dirty work of shouting for

Victor Emmanuel are paid five scudi a day, food and lodging found for them, and in cases where they are too ragged and disgusting to be admitted even into the ranks of their *confrères*, clothing is provided.

The streets are gay with banners, the two United States flags doing duty in friendly embrace with the Italian. The foreign ambassadors of Spain, Portugal, Prussia, Bavaria, Brazil, Turkey, Low Countries, Sweden, Switzerland, United States, and Greece have arrived, but none of them (the Spanish and Portuguese not excepted, and they are *roba di casa*) display their national ensigns, the United States Minister only tacitly allowing the desecration of our national colors.

The English Ambassador is to arrive to-night, but the Russian, Austrian, French and Belgian representatives remain quietly in Florence.

It was amusing to hear this morning, in my walk through the Corso (for I went out quietly to see what was going on), to hear the comments of the *Trasteverini*, who were also on a tour of inspection, upon the style of the various decorations. Workmen were busy nailing up garlands, and squares of white cotton impressed with the arms of the various Italian cities were hung out; later, however, the garlands had been pulled down or had fallen.

The Italian arms and portraits of the King were affixed to many of the palaces of the noble and clerical families, and a *guard stationed to prevent their being taken down!*

The King arrived at half-past twelve, and was escorted to the Quirinal palace amidst the vavats of his hired rabble. The programme of reception was carried out as far as its enforcement could be made.

July 3d, Midnight.—I have just left my father-in-law's chamber for a few hours rest. The physician gives no hope of his recovery. This morning his valet came to me early and told me that on entering the Count's chamber he had found him speechless, and when I went to him I found he had had a stroke. I feared it after the excitement of last evening.

The illumination was quite a failure, and so enraged the mob that they proceeded to take the law into their own hands. In Trastavere there was not a light shown, and the roughs brought ladders to one house *occupied entirely by women,* and hung lanterns up by the outside.

They attempted the same thing with us, but I took two six-shooters in my hands, and giving two others to Pat, my valet, went onto the front balcony, and told them the first one who rested a ladder against the house was a dead man, and when they threatened vengeance, I announced myself a citizen of the United States, and claimed the protection of my country. One of the rabble, bolder than the rest, proceeded, in spite of my protest, to bring up a lantern. I fired, hitting him in the arm, and then, seeing that I was in earnest, they concluded that discretion was the better part of valor, and withdrew, carrying their wounded companion with them.

But this insult was too great a shock to the Count, and we were seriously alarmed about him until a late hour. Ginevra did not leave his bedside until after one o'clock, when he seemed quite disposed to sleep, and in that sleep the stroke must have fallen.

The grand dinner at the Quirinal was a grand fiasco; no ladies were present but the Princess Margharita and her four attendants!

The King refused to sleep at the Quirinal, and passed the night at Prince Doria's.

This morning the Holy Father gave audience to three thousand employees, civil and military, who have refused all allegiance to the Robber, who made a speech to-day in which he announced that he had come to Rome with the *consent of all nations,* not excepting that of *France!*

At the review this afternoon, the wind, they say, played havoc with the decorations of the royal balcony. There were about three thousand troops present out of a body some twenty thousand strong.

JULY 4th.—The Count is still in that terrible state which is neither death nor life, and so infinitely worse than the former!

As soon as I could leave the house, I repaired to the Vatican, in order to inform the Holy Father and the Count's friends there of his state, and ask their prayers.

As I rode along the streets, there were many jeering remarks made at and to me, and one man, who perhaps was among the crowd which has caused our trouble, laid his hand upon my bridle, with some muttered threat, but a sharp cut with my whip caused him to draw back with a howl of pain, and I reached the Vatican without further trouble.

The Holy Father and the Cardinal Secretary were very much distressed by my intelligence, and Cardinal di Santo Giovanni promised, if possible, to pay the Count a visit.

The ball at the Campodoglio announced for 10 P. M. was opened an hour earlier, as his Majesty left at 11. It opened by a *quadrille of honor*, danced by Prince Humbert and the Princess Pallavicini; Syndic Pallavicini and Mde. Pantaleoni; Sir Augustus Paget, the English Ambassador, and the Marquise Lavaggi; the Marquis Origo and Mde. Fratellini; and Cavalier Trocchi and Countess Carpegna.

According to *La Libertà*, the music was bad, ditto the illuminations, and the ladies exceedingly few in number, only four of noble birth being present, of them only one of the highest rank. Altogether the patriotic editor considers the affair totally unworthy of the King of Italy!

JULY 5th.—The Count is still in that terrible state, and poor Ginevra almost heartbroken.

The King left last night, and the foreign Ministers are following him. The city is subsiding, as the rabble are also disappearing.

JULY 6th.—Count Manzano died last night without any return to consciousness.

JULY 10th.—It is all over—the excitements of the funeral and the last arrangements. My poor Ginevra is very, very sad, though very quiet in her grief, and seems to cling now to me with a greater dependence than before. The boy misses his grandfather, and cries frequently for "avo!" "avolo!"

I have arranged to leave Rome for Lucerne, Switzerland, day after to-morrow; to-morrow Ginevra will have a parting audience with the Holy Father.

We will travel through the mountains of Switzerland all summer, and in the fall go aboard the yacht at Nice and repeat our tour of the Mediterranean, making longer visits to the Holy Land and the holy places there.

LUCERNE, July 20th.—We have been here a week, and the change has done Ginevra good already.

The parting interview with the Holy Father was a very sad one. He had known the Count from childhood and been very much attached to him; together they had borne arms in the Guarde Nobile of Pius VII, and their mothers had been dear and intimate friends, although the Countess Mastai-Ferretti was some years the elder.

His Holiness took baby Louis in his arms and blessed him, and the boy was highly delighted with his gold cross and chain, twisting his little fingers in it. But when the Pope spoke to him, he raised his large blue eyes to his face and fixed them there as if fascinated.

The calm serenity of the holy Pontiff is very reassuring. It seems as if he must have (and doubtless he has) a prevision of the end, when all this trouble will be over and the Church once more free.

Well! When shall we see Rome again?

Not certainly while the present diabolical "possession" lasts. And how long that will continue, God in his infinite wisdom only knows!

AUGUST 1st.—We lead a very quiet,

retired life. My time is mostly taken up with Ginevra and endeavoring to distract her from her sorrow. She bears up nobly, and makes every effort to prevent me from feeling gloomy.

And I, too, miss the kindly old man, from whom I can remember nothing but gentleness and fatherly kindness in the four years I have known him. He seemed as it were to take my own father's place so naturally that I grew to feel towards him almost the same affection.

August 1st.—Novara writes that as soon as Eleanore is able to travel he, too, will join us here, expatriating himself as we have done until brighter times dawn for Rome, its ruler, and its people.

Meanwhile it behooves Catholics to gird up their loins and be ready for what may happen—to look to their armor, that the enemy may not surprise them.

And the time has come for Catholics to do away with the amiable complaisance which some, influenced by their natural affections for Protestant friends or relatives, express in regard to those souls. We know that our Blessed Saviour said Himself: "There shall be one fold and one shepherd." "He that hears you hears me." "If they will not hear the Church let them be to thee as the heathen and the publican." What words can be plainer? We may love our "separated brethren" with all our hearts, but mingled with that love must ever be a deep and pitying compassion that so much sincerity and desire to do God's will and follow His commandments should be so wrongly directed and so unavailing.

While, then, we mourn over the sufferings inflicted by the agents of Satan upon Christ's Church and its Head, we also feel an assurance that He will in time cause His spotless bride to triumph over all her enemies and shine out before the world in renewed and redoubled splendor from this the overshadowing sorrow of her present pain. Let us pray for her and for her

Head, that the time of the manifestation of God's glory may be soon; let us also pray as He did upon the cross for his murderers, "Father, forgive them, for they know not what they do;" for those poor wretches who have worked for us so much trouble, and for those who, from a mistaken idea of what true liberty is, applaud and uphold them.

And while firmly planted upon the Rock, against which the gates of hell shall never prevail, if we keep our eyes fixed upon the cross, the storm may beat and the winds may howl, we need not fear, for we will surely feel the truth of the words:

In Hoc Signo Vinces.

THE END.

www.ingramcontent.com/pod-product-compliance
Lightning Source LLC
Chambersburg PA
CBHW022107230426
43672CB00008B/1304